Test Anxiety

& What You Can Do About It

A Practical Guide for Teachers, Parents, and Kids

Joseph Casbarro, Ph.D.

DUDE PUBLISHING
A Division of
National Professional Resources, Inc.
Port Chester, New York

Casbarro, Joseph.
    Test anxiety & what you can do about it : a practical
guide for teachers, parents, and kids / Joseph Casbarro.
    p. cm.
    Includes bibliographical references and index.
    ISBN 1-887943-63-3

    1. Test anxiety. 2. Students—Psychology.
I. Title. II. Title: Test anxiety and what you can do
about it

LB3060.6.C37 2003   371.26'01'9
                                    QBI03-200068

Cover/Book Design & Production by Andrea Cerone, National
Professional Resources, Inc., Port Chester, NY

Dude Publishing
A Division of National Professional Resources, Inc.
25 South Regent Street
Port Chester, New York 10573
Toll free: (800) 453-7461
Phone: (914) 937-8879

Visit our web site: www.NPRinc.com

Printed in the United States of America

ISBN 1-887943-63-3

To Kalyn, Corey and George.
May you never have another sleepless night.

Contents

Chapter 3

Parents, and Teachers and Kids...Oh, My!

Parents, teachers and kids are the stakeholder groups that have the most influence and impact on test anxiety. This chapter provides valuable information about how each group contributes to raising test anxiety.

Chapter 4

Controlling Test Anxiety:
A Framework for Understanding

This chapter provides a framework to address test anxiety in three phases. It also examines valuable theories that can help explain ways to reduce test anxiety in each phase. A model describing the symptoms associated with test anxiety is also presented.

Chapter 5

Pre-Testing Strategies

A series of specific strategies and techniques are provided in this chapter that can be taught and implemented in the pre-testing phase.

Chapter 6
In this chapter, a series of specific strategies and techniques are provided that can be taught in the pre-testing phase, but implemented in the test-in-progress phase.

Chapter 7
After the completion of an exam, test anxiety does not automatically disappear. This chapter addresses the lingering negative effects by providing helpful strategies in the post-testing phase.

Chapter 8
This chapter provides helpful ideas on raising awareness and developing plans to address test anxiety in a purposeful and meaningful way.

Charts

Chart **Title** **Page**

Foreword

With the increased emphasis on testing in vogue now among some educators and many political leaders, the challenge of test anxiety is of paramount importance. As Dr. Casbarro notes, with some alarm, the old achievement and aptitude tests with which many of the baby boom generation are familiar are giving way to a "high stakes" testing movement, often motivated by considerations far removed from the immediate educational needs of our children. Trapped in these cross-currents—indeed, often paralyzed by fear and anxiety—our children may no longer experience schools as safe and supportive environments. Rather, for many, the classroom has become their worst nightmare, in part because it is the setting for the major stressors in their lives.

While this problem might be addressed by questioning the goals of the standards-accountability-testing political movement, it is unlikely that the move toward "evidence-based education" (with its parallel's in medicine, psychotherapy, and the like) is going away any time soon. As such, we must prepare our children for a new kind of educational experience, and one that will require skills to cope with these new stressors. Dr. Casbarro's focus on emotional preparation for testing and the emotional management of testing situations represents a missing set of tools needed to equip our children for the modern classroom. Of course, there is no replacement for good study habits, positive learning attitudes, and hard work. But many children, if they cannot cope with the stresses of testing and other school activities, will underperform their academic potential. And the consequences of such underperformance can ramify throughout their lives.

In a lively, hands-on, and anecdotal way, Joseph Casbarro has written a book that will be of considerable use to parents, educators, and children. He moves easily between the political and educational contexts in which we now find ourselves and the daily experience of students and teachers in the classroom. His approach to test anxiety is well grounded in the scientific literature on the fight-or-flight response; the way in which fear is processed in the brain; optimal levels of arousal; the interplay between cognition, emotion, and action; and coping strategies. And, yet, he is able to provide a wealth of useful, practical tools to address the problem.

Of course, my personal interest in test anxiety generally and in Dr. Casbarro's wonderful book concerns the relation between school stress and Emotional Intelligence. For more than a dozen years, my collaborator John D. Mayer and I have been working on a way of characterizing skills and abilities that help us to recognize emotions in ourselves and others; understand these feelings and use language to communicate them; harness the power of emotion as a tool in cognitive activities like problem-solving, reasoning, and creativity; and manage emotions both in oneself and in other people. (For a review of research on Emotional Intelligence in educational settings see Salovey & Sluyter, 1997; for a more general review see Feldman-Barrett & Salovey, 2002). Of course, it is the latter set of skills—managing emotions— to which coping and overcoming test anxiety belong. Dr. Casbarro does a fine job integrating skills that have to do with appropriate test preparation and test-taking strategy along with those skills more focused on the emotions themselves. In this sense, the book that you are about to read offers an integrative synthesis of the "psychology of tests, testing, and test-taking."

But the really nice thing about *Test Anxiety & What You Can Do About It* is that it goes beyond the psychological level of analysis to also explore what teachers, schools, and school systems can do at the organizational level to help children deal with the rigors of testing. Dr. Casbarro's advice turns parents into therapists, teachers into coaches, and educational administrators into organizational development specialists in order to address this problem. His many charts, grids, and exercises are of enormous help in confronting test anxiety, and they assist us in not over-psychologizing this issue. It appears that tests will long be with us—and that, indeed, when it comes to stressful testing experiences giving rise to intense test anxiety, no child will be left behind! Reading Dr. Casbarro's book and acting on his advice, however, are ways we can help our children to deal with this increasingly salient part of schooling in America and throughout the world.

Peter Salovey, Ph.D.
Dean of the Graduate School of Arts & Sciences
Yale University

Acknowledgments

To Andrea Cerone for her patience, under-standing and outstanding technical skills.

To Helene and Lisa Hanson for their support, guidance and masterful editing.

To Peter Salovey for his kindness, friendship and contribution to the field of Emotional Intelligence.

To the many wonderful teachers, administra-tors, parents and students who taught me so much about the teaching and learning process.

Editor's Note

Dude Publishing, as an imprint of National Professional Resources, Inc., is proud to publish this book, ***Test Anxiety & What You Can Do About It: A Practical Guide for Teachers, Parents, and Kids.*** Our research reveals that this is the first work to directly address the anxiety that emanates from our current focus on testing. We wish to both thank and compliment Dr. Joseph Casbarro for the exemplary way in which he executed this project. It is an honor to have him as a professional colleague and personal friend.

For readers who wish to fully understand the context and issues surrounding test anxiety, Chapters 1 through 3 will be most useful. For those who want to cut to the chase and delve into strategies and techniques, it is recommended that you move directly to Chapter 4.

Whatever your method of travel through the pages that follow, we wish you well in making every aspect of the teaching-learning environment positive and joyful, as well as successful.

Introduction

It is a simple fact. There is just too much anxiety in our lives. Each day it seems that we are finding newer and more creative ways to worry. Some say it's due to the information age, where television and the Internet bring instant news about every real or potential danger in the world into our homes every day.

Regardless of the causes, there's certainly no shortage of things to worry about. Foods that cause cancer, mad cow disease, e-coli bacteria, power lines that emit electromagnetic fields, brain tumors from cell phones, to name just a few. We even worry about things that are designed to help and protect us. Medicines found to have long term side effects, car airbags that kill small children if deployed, and the list goes on.

On top of those worries, add terrorism in the aftermath of September 11th, anthrax, biochemical threats, and dirty bombs. There is little doubt that we are living in an increasingly dangerous world, so why shouldn't we be anxious? And, virtually every walk of life seems to be riddled with greater insecurity and anxiety.

In addition to perceived threats to our health and safety comes an increasing level of worry about our financial security. Will the stock market crash? Are our retirement funds safe? Will social security go bankrupt? Can investors trust corporate executives and audited accounting reports? Even in our most personal relationships we have grown more worrisome. We worry if our marriage will survive or whether our children will have full and happy lives.

What I have found most troubling, and a primary reason that I chose to write this book, is that adults' anxieties and worries are being increasingly transmitted to children. Regardless of the source, it is unfortunate that any adult has to feel highly anxious. But when a young child or adolescent is anxious, it is truly a travesty. Childhood and adolescence should be times of play, fun-filled activities and learning—a worry-free, stress-free existence. "Hakuna Matata" was the term used in Disney's *The Lion King*. If we have to feel anxious, I believe that it should be an "adults only" experience.

I recognize that we cannot control all of the factors that contribute to children's anxieties—their worry about having their tonsils removed, their anxiety about the first day of school, or their worry about the health of a sick friend. Some would argue that as parents our primary job is not to teach, but to *protect* our children. We need to shield them from life's dangers and anxieties. Similarly, those who are employed to teach children are supposed to do it in an emotionally safe and nurturing environment. Then, why have we as a society purposely added more anxiety to the childhood experience? And, why is a major source of that anxiety coming from our homes and our schools?

With the move toward higher standards came a very negative and unintended outcome—anxiety. With higher and more rigorous standards came greater accountability. With greater accountability came more tests. With more tests came more anxiety. We "raised the bar," developed high stakes testing, and created one of the most stress-filled learning environments in history—all in the name of higher standards. We wanted to raise achievement, but in the process we raised anxiety which, as you will see, actually produces the opposite effect.

That is where this book comes in. It is intended to be a valuable resource designed to enlighten educators, parents, and students to the causes and symptoms of test anxiety. More importantly, it will provide effective strategies and techniques to reduce test anxiety's negative effects.

If readers of this book say that it is just *common sense*, then I will be pleased. Too much common sense is missing today from our educational system. However, if after reading this book educators, parents, and students develop plans to routinely incorporate strategies to reduce test anxiety as part of their preparation for high stakes tests, then I will know that my objective has been met.

The purpose of this book is to create in every classroom and home across America a commitment to test preparation that goes beyond drilling for content and taking practice tests. One that addresses emotional preparation. To create in every home and school a positive and supportive environment where students appropriately study and take tests knowing that their parents and teachers will still love them the morning after—regardless of their scores. To help students take control of their fears so that they can perform at their best, knowing that they are worthwhile human beings, no matter what the test results reveal.

Although the focus is on grades K - 12, this book covers a considerable amount of information that is applicable from elementary school through college. The primary focus is on what are called norm-referenced standardized tests and high stakes state-mandated tests. However, the strategies and techniques can apply to all tests including teacher-made local exams.

I tried to write this book in an easy-to-read, conversational manner, not as a textbook. In doing so, my hope is that the material covered becomes part of every teacher's, parent's, and student's toolbox, so that the array of practical ideas and strategies presented can be pulled out and used as needed to lower the high anxiety that so often contributes to lower test performance. There is a glossary of terms as well as appendices of valuable information in the back of the book.

Test Anxiety & What You Can Do About It is just the beginning of the journey. In future editions, I hope to add other strategies collected from individuals from all over the country. Please e-mail me at *testanxiety@nprinc.com* if you would like to make a contribution to my future work, or to offer any feedback on how this book has helped you, your students, or your child.

Sit back, enjoy, and most importantly, don't worry. I assure that there will be no test at the end!

Chapter 1
"Daddy, Daddy, I Can't Sleep"

About two years ago, on a very stormy night, my wife and I went to bed late. I remember that the wind was blowing quite fiercely outside of our bedroom window. I tossed and turned until I finally fell asleep. At about three o'clock in the morning, I awoke to an unusual sound. At first, I thought it was the wind. But the wind had stopped blowing. Then I thought I was dreaming, but the sound kept getting louder. My wife shook me and said, "I think it's one of the kids. Get up and go check them."

As I got up and moved toward our bedroom door, I could tell that the sound was coming from our daughter Kalyn's bedroom. As I approached her room, I began to distinguish the sound. It was my daughter's voice saying, "Daddy, can you come here? Daddy, Daddy, I can't sleep."

I went into her room, sat on the edge of her bed and asked, "Kalyn, what's the matter?" At first no answer. I asked if her head or stomach hurt her. Kalyn said, "No." I felt her forehead...no temperature. Once again, I asked, "What's wrong?"

Finally, after I had held her tightly, she said, "I'm

worried about tomorrow's test. I can't sleep. I keep thinking about it. I want to pass it."

What was so strange about her response was that Kalyn, being an excellent student, had never lost sleep over schoolwork or tests. She is not a worrier. She had always been, and continues to be, a sound sleeper. Once to bed, she always sleeps through the night.

What I had forgotten about was the new test she was to take the next day. Kalyn was nine years old at that time and in 4th grade. She was scheduled to take a new state mandated test in English/Language Arts that her school and schools throughout the area had been preparing to administer. For months before this test, kids were taking sample tests. Across the state, school principals were advising parents about the importance of doing well on these exams. Teachers were converting classrooms into test prep centers. PTAs were holding meetings to explain the new tests to parents. Newspapers were eagerly awaiting the results to be released.

After consoling my daughter, I kissed her and tucked her in. I went back to our bedroom where my wife inquired how she was doing. When I told her about Kalyn's anxiety about taking the test, or should I say her anxiety about *doing well* on the test, she reminded me of a letter we had received from school the previous week.

The letter instructed us to make sure that our child went to bed early the night before the test, and to provide a good breakfast on the morning of the test. Clearly the school wanted students to perform well, as the test results would reflect upon the quality of the school and the district. It never mentioned that anxiety might be a factor.

Prior to that night we had never spoken to Kalyn

about the significance of this test. In fact, we had tried to down play the test. However, we didn't need to emphasize its importance because she *knew* from the actions of adults in the school and from her friends that this test was really important.

I remember saying to my wife before getting back into bed that something is seriously wrong when nine year old kids are losing sleep over a test. After all, this wasn't the Law Boards or even the SAT.

How many children lie awake each night worrying about tomorrow's test? Unfortunately, too many, I suspect.

Valuing High Stakes Tests

Like guilt, anxiety is a man-made emotion. Here we are in an enlightened society in the 21st century, yet the amount of stress we put on our children is ridiculous. The term "high stakes" not only refers to the importance that we give to a child's performance on a test, but also to the increased pressure our society places on the *value* of the test itself. It is almost as if the total worth of our schools is dependent on performing well on these tests.

After all, we must realize that only one purpose of these tests is to determine *how well* students are doing and *which* students need help. The other purposes have more to do with politics and comparing one school or district to another, identifying strong and weak schools, and maybe even real estate values!

If I sound bias, it is because I am. There is certainly a role for assessments and tests, but not at the expense of what we value most. Teaching should instill a love of learning. And learning should be fun, creative, and exciting. It should be measured in many different ways. Kids should want to go to school and leave their fears and anxieties elsewhere. Their gifts and talents should be nurtured. I guess you could say that I'm a romantic about teaching and learning.

That being said, I'm also a realist. Otherwise, why would I write a book about test anxiety instead of one about the dangers of standardized testing? However, I think that is better left to others, like Alfie Kohn and Peter Sacks, who have written so well on this topic.

Alfie Kohn, author of *Punished By Rewards, The Schools Our Children Deserve* and *The Case Against Standardized Testing*, is a leading crusader and very controversial figure in the debate over testing. In some educational circles he is portrayed as the villain because he is challenging the value of standardized tests in a political climate where they are thriving. To others he is the hero because they believe that the high stakes, high accountability movement is ruining our schools. Regardless of where you fall on the issue of standardized and high stakes tests, Alfie Kohn is definitely required reading, because he forces you to think deeply about what you value.

Alfie Kohn has identified five fatal flaws in the so-called "standards movement," a movement that places emphasis on standardized testing to measure students' progress.

First, he argues that there is a preoccupation with achievement in our schools that can lead to the wrong types of motivation. He argues that instead of motivating students to learn, the emphasis on achievement actually has the opposite effect. By undermining their interest in learning and leading them to avoid challenging themselves, students' goals become doing well on tests rather than focusing on the quality of their learning.

Second, Kohn talks about the impact that the standards movement has had on what he calls "old school teaching"—the sort of instruction that treats kids more as empty vessels that are to be filled with knowledge, where the teacher is the "sage on the stage" instead of a facilitator or guide. The focus becomes coverage of content rather than teaching for understanding. He emphasizes that this type of teaching encourages high achieving students to remember only long enough to pass tests, while it discourages low achieving students from learning at all.

Third, Kohn contends that the standards movement has become totally wedded to standardized testing in an effort to address the accountability issue, and to ensure that students are meeting these higher, more rigorous standards. He argues that the more tests are used as a basis of promoting or retaining students, or for funding or closing down schools, the more anxiety will rise and the less valid the scores become.

Fourth, the standards movement has consisted of imposing specific requirements in an effort to coerce improvement. This top-down pressure from political and governmental leaders through the various state education departments is causing tremendous stress on schools and school systems. Kohn argues that coercive approaches, such as rewarding schools with high test scores and punishing schools with poor test scores, are doomed to failure. They ultimately force good people out of education, and those that remain are reduced to finding blame when test scores drop (blame the teachers, blame the parents, blame the kids).

Fifth, and finally, the standards movement, according to Kohn, can be summarized in three words—harder is better. There is the presumption that if we make the standards harder and more difficult, and "raise the bar," we will ultimately create an environment that is better for our children

to learn in. He argues that the proponents of tougher standards and high stakes testing often want to do more of the
same. Give students more homework. Make school longer.
Test them more often. In fact, several states have shortened
summer vacations and started the school year early in order
to get a head start on preparing for state mandated tests.
Poor performance on these tests can mean millions of lost
dollars in federal money, as will be discussed later in this
chapter.

Peter Sacks, author of *Standardized Minds*, explores
three myths that have given rise to America's love affair with
high stakes testing and school accountability:

Myth #1:   American schools are in peril.

Myth #2:   The US economy is in peril because of
an inferior educational system.

Myth #3:   Greater school "accountability" will mean
higher achievement.

Sacks' articulate and well researched presentation explains
how the Nation At-Risk Report in the early 1980's became a
political movement to link the potential failure of the US
economy to our school systems' perceived deficiencies.
That linkage drove initiatives over the last three presidential
administrations to focus on greater school accountability
through higher learning standards and increased testing. I
wonder if the weakness in the American economy early in
this 21st century is actually due to failing schools. I haven't
heard anyone blame the Japanese school system for the
economic problems in that country. Sacks helps us better
understand how this politically popular movement over the
past decade has contributed to higher school accountability
that he believes does not lead to higher educational quality.

My goal is not to debate the political and philosophical arguments about high stakes testing. It is to help educators, parents, and students cope with the increasing amounts of test anxiety prevalent in our society today as a result of these high stakes tests. If Alfie Kohn, Peter Sacks, and their disciples are successful in their crusade to reduce or eliminate high stakes testing, I could then possibly turn my attention to writing about other, more interesting topics in the field of education. Needless to say, my publisher and I believe that high stakes testing and its associated anxieties will be around for quite a bit longer. If not, we would not have invested so much in this publication.

Be careful. Remember, our behavior as adults defines what we value, so we must be very thoughtful in what we *do* and in what we *say* around this very important topic of high stakes testing. Little did I ever realize how our daughter's sleepless night would be the experience of so many parents around the country.

The Explosion of Testing

Recently, there has been much in the news about access to nuclear weapons and how terrorist states could obtain either the weapons themselves, or the nuclear material used to manufacture them.

I can't help but think of how the proliferation of these weapons during the cold war era was viewed as a *necessary* evil. The United States and the then U.S.S.R. had to match weapon for weapon, warhead for warhead, in order for each super power to feel safe. I remember how the Cuban missile crisis shook our nation when I was a child. The arms race became a perceived deterrent to world war, or so the argument went.

As we look at what is now perceived to be a crisis in confidence in our public school system, there appears to be a proliferation of testing. While I'm not suggesting that the dangers of testing have any correlation to the dangers of nuclear weapons, the premise or rationale underlying testing's widespread use does.

Just like national security during the cold war, education has become one of our country's top political priorities. Our government does not really trust schools to report on their own progress so it has developed a closely monitored, state controlled system to measure the performance of schools. And state testing systems, like nuclear silos, have risen up across the country.

Although the President and federal government are promoting testing at the end of every grade starting in Grade 3, the primary responsibility for the increase in testing rests with state education departments. Most states have embarked on massive statewide testing programs, not only at the high school level for graduation where it had been for years, but also at the middle and elementary school levels.

Testing has gone from a cottage industry to big business. District-by-district, school-by-school, and state-by-state analyses are made in various professional publications and in the media at large. Like MAD (Mutually Assured Destruction), testing programs have grown to such an extent that in some key grades, like 8th grade, students are taking so many state mandated tests that classroom instruction virtually ends a month early with the last weeks of school reserved just for review and testing.

It is this proliferation, based on a need for data-driven accountability, that has contributed to the rise in test anxiety in our society. The tests are often viewed as *necessary evils*, since we seem to have no better way to objectively measure student performance across grades, schools, districts, and states.

And, like nuclear weapons, we will not stop deploying tests until we as a society feel secure and confident enough in our school systems to do so. Unfortunately, like the history of the cold war, elaborate state mandated testing programs are likely to be here for a long time to come.

Protests around the country, like those in the 60's against nuclear proliferation, have sprung up against standardized testing. Often they have occurred in high socio-economic areas where parents and educators view these state tests as unnecessary and not helpful in measuring achievement. These are communities with top performing schools, where the state mandated tests actually measure skills below those set at the local level. Furthermore, it is argued that these tests are not needed to identify students with special learning needs since these districts believe that they already have systems in place to do this more effectively. These districts also want the states to give more choices in the types of tests used, as well as in the testing formats.

Often, in poorer socio-economic areas, the results of these state testing systems have become very threatening. The results lead to identifying and targeting schools in need of technical assistance and ultimately to closing schools down entirely. Imagine the stress and anxiety on everyone associated with a school that has been historically a poor performer. So the temptation is for everyone to teach *to* the test.

Teaching to the Test

One of the most overused and misunderstood concepts associated with the growth of testing programs is *teaching to the test*. What exactly does this mean? Is it a good thing or a bad thing to do? Let me explain.

We can all agree that driving a car is a very serious responsibility. It is literally a matter of life and death. So to ask prospective drivers to demonstrate their skills on the road and to be evaluated by a professional from the Department of Motor Vehicles makes a lot of sense. You need to practice left turns, right turns, three point turns, and that knee-knocking parallel park. If you are taking a driver's test to obtain your license, you had better be taught to the test.

Furthermore, anyone who has taught his or her 16-year-old to drive, as I did this past year, knows that you try to include all of the important parts of driving in your teaching—putting on your seatbelt, adjusting the mirrors, watching your speed, etc. I was literally teaching skills that were to be assessed as part of the upcoming road test. So, I was teaching to the test and proud of it. And it paid off—my son passed!

So why is the term *teaching to the test* often used in such a derogatory and negative way? The answer has more to do with *what* the test is about and what it purports to measure, rather than teaching *to* it. When we talk about the kinds of tests that are given as part of many state mandated programs, we're referring to tests that are not as authentic as a driver's road test. By that I mean that the tests do not always measure the skills as directly and in real life situations. For example, they're often only paper and pencil tests.

As a society, we have determined that the written 25-item multiple choice test used to obtain a driver's permit is not adequate to obtain a driver's license. The written test helps to determine if someone knows the rules of the road, but it is insufficient in determining if someone can safely drive a car. The same is true in school.

Most states have well defined learning standards that range from reading, writing, and arithmetic, to character education. In order to know how well students can read or do math, we ask them to demonstrate it. Every day in class, as well as through various projects and homework assignments, students must read aloud and/or silently, write book reports on what they have read, do math problems in class or on a worksheet for homework, and the like. So when it comes time for a test, they should be well prepared. And, usually they are—for their teacher's made tests. The teacher knows what has been taught. Hopefully he/she has made the expectations for learning clear, and the students have a good idea what is going to be on the test, including the format of the test itself.

However, when a test is constructed far away from a student's particular classroom by individuals who do not know these students or their teacher, there is a greater chance of problems. In this case, instead of the teacher and the students knowing exactly how the test will reflect the content, they must first get a sample of the test to find out. Does what they have been doing in class match what will be on the test? Namely, is what the teacher has been teaching consistent with what will be covered on the test? This match between instruction, curriculum and assessment is called *alignment.*

To complicate the situation further, one cannot make the assumption that if the curriculum being taught is aligned with the standards the test will automatically be aligned. The reason is there are many different ways to assess competence or mastery of a learning standard. Through projects, cooperative learning assignments, class presentations, portfolios, and the like, teachers can measure a student's progress toward the learning standard. Once the number of options available to demonstrate proficiency are reduced, students' ability to succeed, and/or demonstrate their skills is narrowed.

If a test is only a paper and pencil exercise, then it significantly limits the ways that a student can demonstrate what he/she knows. Additionally, standardized tests place time constraints on students that increase the pressure to perform and often contribute to raising anxiety. Going back to our example of a written permit test versus a hands-on road test, there is no debate. The closer the assessment is to what is to be measured, the better and more accurate the assessment. In other words, the more *authentic* the measure, the better the instrument in assessing what has been learned.

The problem with teaching to the test for many standardized norm-referenced tests is that there is a serious question on the part of many educational professionals themselves as to whether these tests are good measures of the learning standards that they are teaching toward.

If the learning standard relates to students' ability to express themselves verbally, how does a paper and pencil test measure that? But, if the standard is related to how well a student can read a passage and answer comprehension questions, then the test may be a better measure of reading skills. The following chart identifies factors that can increase or decrease the likelihood that teachers will specifically teach to the test.

If the content of the test is different from the curriculum being taught in the class, the likelihood of teaching to the test greatly increases. If the test differs in format from

Chart I

Teaching to the Test

	Increases Likelihood	Decreases Likelihood
Content of test	Not consistent with curriculum being taught	Consistent with curriculum being taught
Format of test	Significantly different from the types of assignments given in class	Similar to the types of classroom and homework assignments given
Nature of the test	Fact-based, memorization type assessment	Problem-solving and more open-ended assessment

the types of quizzes and tests that the teacher usually gives in class, teaching to the test is likely to increase. Also, the more a test measures specific fact-based types of information, the greater the likelihood that teaching to the test will occur.

Teaching to the test can serve to reduce anxiety in that it prepares students for the exam. It helps them better recognize what is expected and gives examples of the items that will appear on the test. In that sense, it is a good thing.

But when teaching to the test becomes the primary goal of instruction in the weeks and months leading up to an important test, it can actually contribute to increased anxiety. First, the overemphasis on test preparation sends a very strong message to the students that the upcoming test is very important. Otherwise, why would we be spending so much time on practice tests?

Second, if a class is spending the majority of its instructional time getting ready for a test, then it is understandable that some parents may become concerned. Everyone (teacher, student and parent) becomes *consumed* by the upcoming test.

Perhaps the biggest criticism of teaching to the test is that it eats into valuable classroom time that many argue should be devoted to quality instruction—not to the review and memorization of facts primarily designed to achieve high test scores.

No Child Left Behind—Test Them All

Testing itself can be a very anxiety provoking experience. Add on top of that the fact that a student has a learning disability, attention deficit disorder, or is a second language learner, and you can move from anxiety to panic!

Commensurate with federal law and most state testing programs are efforts to ensure that all students are tested regardless of disability or language challenge, beginning generally in third grade. The rationale is worthy. Namely, all students need to work toward the same learning standards and be assessed using the same instruments. We do not want to perpetuate what has been a two-track system – one for general education, and a less demanding one for students with special needs.

Several years ago the reauthorization of the Individuals with Disabilities Education Act (IDEA) had placed a strong emphasis on all students with disabilities having equal access to the general education curriculum in the least restrictive environment (LRE). Students with disabilities should be educated with their non-disabled peers to the maximum extent possible using supplementary aids and services, as needed. These students are then assessed based on the general education curriculum.

When it comes to mandated standardized testing, students with disabilities under IDEA or another federal law, Section 504 of the Rehabilitation Act, may be entitled to testing modifications (See Chapter 6: Test-in-Progress Strategies). These testing modifications are designed to accommodate for aspects of their disability that may adversely (and presumably unfairly) affect their ability to perform. For example, extended time for students with reading or processing problems, separate testing locations for students highly distracted by environmental stimuli, large print versions of tests for the visually impaired, and the like.

These modifications, in an era of increased formalized assessments, can greatly help to reduce everyone's anxiety associated with the testing of students with disabilities. This includes parents who fear that their son or daughter will fail the test without accommodations, teachers who know that without specific accommodations students who normally struggle with paper and pencil tasks in class are not likely to perform well, and, of course, the students themselves who recognize that they need a fighting chance to pass a test that may otherwise penalize them for their specific disability.

The most recent federal legislation that is having the greatest impact on school districts across the nation is called the No Child Left Behind (NCLB) Act. Passed in January, 2002, this sweeping legislation mandates that all children (elementary and secondary age) must meet higher, more rigorous standards over the next 12 years. NCLB mandates annual tests in grades 3 through 8 (and one year in 10th - 12th grade) in Reading/Language Arts and Math, and in the 2007-08 school year in Science (for selected grade spans). States must assess each school year and incrementally "raise the bar" each subsequent school year until 100% of all students are performing at proficient levels by the year 2014. These targets include all subgroups as well, such as the economically disadvantaged (Title I), students with disabilities (IDEA and Section 504), Limited English Proficient (LEP) students, as well as students from each racial or ethnic group.

This very ambitious law also imposes financial sanctions if school districts do not meet the state targets. The sanctions include the withholding of federal funds, allowing parents to transfer students to a higher performing school within the district, replacing district personnel and/or changing the governance arrangements. Accountability is the main component of NCLB, with the provision that requires the issuance of state and local district report cards showing aggregate test information on all students, as well as disaggregated data by race, ethnicity, gender, disability status, LEP and status as economically disadvantaged.

In case you are a college student or professor, don't relax. Yes, the focus has been K-12, but that may be changing. There is much discussion about the reauthorization of the federal Higher Education Act which may include some of the same provisions as NCLB. In fact, several public university systems are already beginning to phase in state assessments. Imagine not moving on to the next academic school year without passing mandated tests given by the state. Or, imagine colleges and universities not receiving state or federal aid because of poor test results.

Now that I have your attention, maybe you can understand why anxiety is likely to be a major factor for all stakeholders in our schools. And, more importantly, why we must control it so as to help our students perform at their best.

Chapter 2
Test Anxiety:
A Man-Made Emotion

To better understand anxiety, we need to first distinguish the differences between anxiety and fear. The following story emphasizes the distinction:

A young man from Illinois named Jeremy had always wanted to go on a safari to hunt wild animals. He saved his money and booked a trip to travel to one of the deepest parts of Africa.

On the third day of this safari, the vehicle that carried him and his party stalled out after crossing a creek, and they were stranded for several hours. While they were waiting for help to arrive, they walked toward a heavily wooded area to explore some wildlife.

For some reason Jeremy wandered away from his group. Minutes later he heard a noise coming from a cliff about 80 feet behind him. A lion had spotted him and began running down the cliff at full force toward him. The sight and sound literally paralyzed Jeremy and he couldn't move. He tried to scream, but nothing seemed to come out. He began to shake and realized that if he tried to run, he would never escape this animal. His life flashed before his eyes. Absolute and total panic consumed him.

Just as the lion was about to attack him, two shots rang out from the rifle of the guide leading the safari. The lion laid dead literally at Jeremy's feet. Jeremy then collapsed and was brought back to consciousness by smelling salts. This is an example of fear.

About a year later, as Jeremy was sitting in his lounge chair in his air-conditioned family room back in Illinois, he was changing channels on his television set. He came upon a show sponsored by *National Geographic*. Suddenly and unexpectedly, a lion appeared on the screen. Jeremy began to shake and sweat profusely. His heart rate jumped and he closed his eyes. He wasn't even able to push the button on the remote control to shut off the TV. This is an example of anxiety.

What Is Anxiety?

What's the difference between Jeremy's original fear and his anxiety one year later? The physiological responses were virtually the same, yet the threats that caused the responses were absolutely different. The danger in Africa was real—there was a concrete reason to be fearful. In fact, fear can often help mobilize the body to react. The famous *fight or flight* phenomenon. Although in this case, Jeremy froze like "a deer caught in the headlights." But sitting in the comfort and safety of his air-conditioned home, Jeremy had no rational reason to fear. The lion, after all, was on television. There was no way the animal could hurt him.

Most people would understand and empathize with Jeremy. He had been through a traumatic real-life event that was indelibly imprinted in his memory banks. We would say that his fear of lions was understandable, just as someone who was in an airplane crash would be fearful of flying, or someone who almost drowned would be afraid of water.

But how do we explain why so many people have fears of things with which they never have had a traumatic experience? People who have never touched or been bitten by snakes fear them. Many young people have fears of public speaking although they never have been asked to do it. Many adults can not even take a traditional MRI because they fear enclosed spaces. Most were never trapped in a mine or elevator, but they cannot bear being in the enclosed space of an MRI.

Some of these situational anxieties create significant problems in life because they reduce our effectiveness and our ability to function. They can move from situational anxieties to full-fledged phobias, where the feelings are so intense that they lead to total avoidance of the object or situation. These feelings are so powerful that the mere thought of the feared object or situation can trigger a panic attack.

It is a lot easier to avoid snakes or lions than it is to avoid tests, especially if you are in school. So, anxiety associated with test-taking can create problems. If this situational anxiety escalates into a phobia, then there is an even greater problem.

Considerable research over the past century has contributed to a better understanding of anxiety and its effects. From the studies of Jersild & Holmes in the 1930's to Suinn in the 1960's, the best way to differentiate fear from anxiety is to recognize that fear is initiated by an outside event in the environment and is the body's response to this real threat in the environment. The person experiencing the fear is very aware of its cause, and the intensity of response is usually proportionate to the threat. Also, fear is temporary and acute. Once the real threat is gone, so is the fear.

Chart II

The Differences Between Fear & Anxiety

Fear	Anxiety
• Initiated by an outside event (objective)	• Initiated by internal feelings (subjective)
• Response to a *real* danger/threat	• Response to a *perceived* threat
• Aware of the cause	• Not always aware of the cause
• Intensity of response is proportional to the real danger	• Intensity of response is not proportional to the perceived threat
• Temporary & acute	• Persistent & chronic

Anxiety, on the other hand, is initiated by internal feelings, and it is a response to a *perceived* threat. The cause of the feeling of anxiety is not always known to the person. It tends to be more general. In fact, the intensity of response to anxiety is usually disproportionate to the perceived threat. Rather than being temporary and acute, anxiety is persistent and chronic.

Anxiety plays a very large role in our lives. We worry about many more things today than in past generations, even though our worries have less to do with our survival. We have financial worries, job worries, relationship worries, health worries, and on and on.

What is most troubling to me is that these worries are being transmitted (in word and in action) to our children. They are becoming overly anxious, and one of the most obvious examples is the increase in test anxiety and other anxieties related to doing well in school.

The Origins of Test Anxiety

Are kids born with a fear of tests? In fact, does any newborn have genetically endowed fears or anxieties – fears of snakes, or heights, or small spaces? How about the fear of speaking in front of groups?

I suppose we could begin our discussion with the age-old debate of nature vs. nurture. But that might be too simplistic. Most people believe that both our genetic structure as well as our environmental upbringing contribute to *who* we are and *what* we will become. While the extent to which nature versus nurture contribute to test anxiety is unclear, it is certain that regardless of any predisposition, what we do as adults greatly influences the anxiety that kids feel.

Two domains influence test anxiety: (1) an *individual's characteristics*, and (2) the *environments* in which the individual lives, plays, and works. Although these two domains seem to be related to the nature vs. nurture distinction, I am not looking at the root causes of test anxiety and will not debate whether these environments influence an individual's disposition or vice versa. Knowing that both domains are important influences on test anxiety is, however, very important.

An Individual's Characteristics

In Domain #1 (Individual's Characteristics) there are three factors related to past experiences that influence test anxiety. First, an individual's feeling of self-worth as a student is critically important in dealing with test anxiety. If an individual feels that he/she is not a good student, and has information from past experiences that reinforces that perception, then the possibility of it becoming a self-fulfilling prophecy increases.

Second, confidence or lack of confidence in a specific subject area influences test anxiety. A student can feel that he/she is good in history and in English, but may not feel as competent in math or science. This more targeted type of perception can lead to difficulties in that content area. It can be viewed as a subset of an individual's self-worth, only much more specific.

Third, the ability to regulate one's emotions when confronted with high levels of stress or uncertainty is extremely important in Domain #1. If an individual tends to be very emotional in stressful situations, he/she is more apt to have difficulty in testing situations. Regulating one's emotions is exceedingly important in preparing for and successfully passing high stakes tests. Much more on this aspect will be covered when we talk about Emotional Intelligence in Chapter 4.

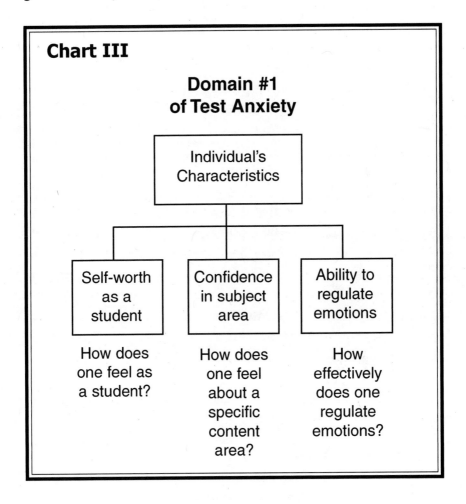

Chart III

**Domain #1
of Test Anxiety**

Individual's
Characteristics

Self-worth as a student	Confidence in subject area	Ability to regulate emotions
How does one feel as a student?	How does one feel about a specific content area?	How effectively does one regulate emotions?

Knowing that one is poor at math or having failed a math test before could help mobilize oneself to study hard and prepare for the test, or it could result in a person saying, "I am not going to study, I always fail my math tests." The decision to study or not may be affected greatly by the environments in which the student operates.

The Environments

Domain #2 (Environments) focuses on the places that individuals must negotiate every day as part of their existence—where they live, work, and play. For students, school is where they work. The school environment in our new era of data driven accountability can become a breeding ground for test anxiety. The more pressure that schools place on students to achieve high test scores, the greater the likelihood that test anxiety will rise.

The home is also a critical environment since parental influence and child rearing can profoundly affect anxiety. In Chapter 3 we will explore parenting styles that adversely impact test anxiety in children. There is little doubt that from a child's earliest ages, parents establish an environment that either raises or lowers their child's anxiety.

Lastly, the community-at-large, including the playground, social gathering places, and the media also play a pivotal role since this is where peer influences and peer pressure have great effect. As students get older, how their peers feel about school and tests can become strong influences on their behavior.

The impact of each of the environments in Domain #2 is dependent on the time spent by the individual in these environments, as well as the importance or significance of the people who inhabit them. It must be noted that the interplay between an individual's characteristics and these environments is critically important. For example, how an individual regulates his emotions may be dependent on the stressors present in the home, school or community environment. The more stress present, the greater the opportunity to develop effective coping skills or possibly the opposite. An individual could become overwhelmed and ineffective in managing the stress.

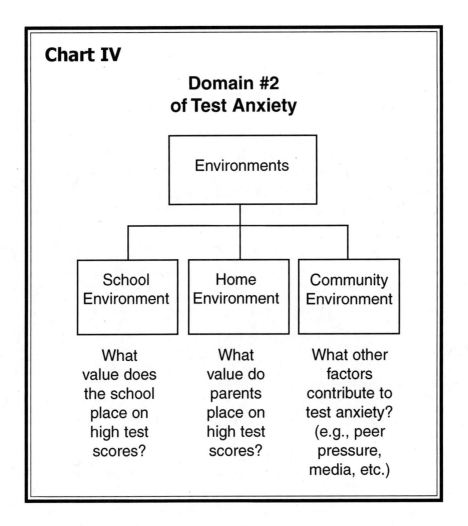

Chart IV

**Domain #2
of Test Anxiety**

Environments

School Environment	Home Environment	Community Environment
What value does the school place on high test scores?	What value do parents place on high test scores?	What other factors contribute to test anxiety? (e.g., peer pressure, media, etc.)

An Optimal Level of Anxiety

The influences of a student's environments are not positive or negative in themselves. It is how the individual's characteristics interact with these environments that will result in the raising or lowering of test anxiety. Does the student want to please his/her parents or not? Do well for his/her teacher or not? Impress his/her friends or not?

While test anxiety can have detrimental effects on performance, it can also be positive, as a *normal* level of anxiety can actually be motivational.

For example, if you do not want to be late for an interview for a new job, you might set the alarm clock the night before, which is a *prudent* thing to do. However, if you wake up every hour during the night to check whether the alarm is set, then you have a problem. Namely, you do not sleep well. You may get to the appointment on time, but your heightened anxiety about waking up on time has actually made you less effective at the interview.

The same thing applies to tests and test-taking. Teachers and parents want students to study for a test, so they emphasize its importance and help students study and prepare. After all, that's the *prudent* thing to do. But students should not be so anxious that they spend all night waking up worrying about the test, like our daughter Kalyn did. Students should be anxious enough to take notes in class and study with classmates, but not so anxious that they make themselves sick with worry. Like the alarm clock analogy, students with too much anxiety will end up taking the test, but not doing their best. Therefore, there is an optimal level of test anxiety, that is strong enough so as to motivate students to try to do their very best by preparing and studying. It is only when the level of anxiety becomes too low or too high that problems begin to develop.

If the test anxiety level in an environment is too low, then teachers will not prepare their students well. In turn, students will not study and parents won't care about the results. If test anxiety is too high, then teachers will over-emphasize the test's importance. In turn, students will cram and become overly anxious regarding the test and parents will worry about the results. More importantly, test performance will suffer.

I refer to test anxiety as a man-made, or stated in a more gender correct fashion, a *person-made* emotion because the level of test anxiety can be influenced in large part by the people in the environment. If we live in a world where teachers are paid more if their students score higher on a test, we have a problem. Or in a world where principals get bonuses for the highest test scores in a district, we have a problem. Or in a world where parents believe that their child's worth is based on the scores they get on standardized tests, then we really have a problem.

Chart V

Levels of Anxiety

Level	Characterized by:
Low	• Little emphasis on test preparation • Limited time on reviewing content • Test results not viewed as important
Optimal	• Appropriate amount of test preparation • Adequate levels of content review • Test results viewed as important
High	• Excessive emphasis on test preparation • Constant preoccupation with upcoming test • Massive time spent on studying ("cramming") • Test results viewed as extremely important

Of course, no teacher, school administrator, or parent is going to directly acknowledge that a child's performance on a test is a true measure of that individual's worth. However, kids are smart. They know what's important and what isn't by recognizing what we, the adults in their lives, value. So, if adults (teachers, principals, parents) spend a great deal of time preparing for tests, giving tests, and celebrating high achievement on these tests, what will kids learn? They learn that tests are important. The results tell if I am smart or not. And if I do not do well, it is embarrassing or worse—I must be dumb. After all, I do not want to let my parents or teachers down. Thus even more anxiety is created.

So, kids learn from an early age that tests matter. Their individual characteristics and the environments that they negotiate work together to create levels of anxiety that at times may be too high or too low. Our goal is to achieve an optimal level of anxiety wherever possible, by utilizing practical strategies and techniques.

Chapter 3
Parents, and Teachers, and Kids...Oh, My!

The more stress that students feel in their lives, the more likely that they will experience heightened levels of test anxiety. In the children's classic *The Wizard of Oz*, Dorothy exclaims, "Lions, and tigers, and bears...oh, my!" as she expresses her fears of what may be some of the dangers on the way to the Emerald City in the Land of Oz. Similarly, we should think about the fears and dangers on our way along the yellow brick road to the land of standardized tests. Parents, and teachers, and kids...oh, my!

That's right. We should fear each of these individual groups as Dorothy feared lions, tigers, and bears. The reason is that each stakeholder group can significantly contribute to heightening levels of test anxiety.

Parents (as Stakeholders)...

One day I was having lunch with a friend of mine who is a psychiatrist working at a prestigious psychiatric hospital. I told him that I was in the midst of writing a book on test anxiety. His response was swift and to the point. He said, "I hope that you are going to address parents. They are a major contributor to this problem." Why does everyone from psychiatrists to teachers point to the parents? And why would parents knowingly contribute to high levels of test anxiety? After all, parents want their children to be happy, well adjusted students who achieve in school, don't they?

As was stated earlier, parents begin by reinforcing how important tests are at an early age. They communicate, often unintentionally, that how well people do on tests is a function of intelligence. They reinforce this message by becoming wrapped up in the prevailing societal view that smart kids are the ones who score well on tests.

Also, as parents are the most significant individuals in a young child's life, children often want to please them. They want to do well, whether it is in school, sports or other activities, to seek the approval, acceptance, and love of their parents. It is only later in childhood and adolescence that kids learn that they should perform well for themselves.

At a young age, doing well is more about winning parental approval than it is about self esteem. In fact, a young child's self esteem is often defined by how proud he/she makes his/her parents. Most parents seem to recognize this power and assure their children that they are loved and accepted regardless of performance when it comes to areas outside of school. If a child's little league team loses and their child did not score a run, they say, "We are still proud of you. We love you. You will do better next time."

But, for many parents there is less acceptance when their child does not do well in school. In such cases parents tend to attribute blame to either the child (Blame the Child Syndrome), or the school (Blame the School Syndrome).

Blame the Child Syndrome

Blame the Child Syndrome has two distinct patterns of parental behavior. Parents either feel that their child is lazy or unmotivated, or they feel that something is wrong with their child.

When parents feel that their child is lazy or unmotivated, they often try to coerce the child into studying more. "No TV or video games until your homework is finished." "You can't play with your friends after school until you do your homework." "No new bicycle until you start doing better in school." This coercion is intended to be helpful, not mean or punitive. In other words, parents love their children and view such coersion as part of their parental responsibility to "crack the whip" (figuratively, not literally) when their child is not on the right path.

No matter how painful it may be, parents often feel the need to threaten and punish to gain their child's attention and compliance. And guess what? It works. Well, at least for a short while. The problem is, it does not work for long.

In the best seller, *Punished By Rewards*, Alfie Kohn explains how we use rewards as a means of coercion. Kohn offers that just because parents pride themselves on giving so-called positive reinforcement, does not make it less coercive. Parents are still "pulling the strings" and attempting to control and influence their child's behavior *extrinsically*. The real concern with any type of behavior modification is that it may hinder children from ultimately developing the intrinsic motivation to do well in school.

The second pattern of Blame the Child Syndrome is quite the opposite. Instead of seeing the child as lazy and unmotivated, the child is viewed as a victim. In other words, the child is not responsible for poor performance because of a problem over which he/she has little or no control—a learning disability, a processing problem, an attention disorder, a hyperactivity disorder, etc.

In this pattern, the parent is more apt to become an *enabler* than a punisher. The parent will try to find explanations for the child's poor performance that relate to a perceived or real problem or disability. In doing so, the child may not be held accountable for poor performance. "How can he/she do well in school when he/she is unable to focus?" "How could we expect him/her to pass this timed test when he/she is so distractible?" (Refer to The Victim parenting type in a later part of this chapter.)

This component of the syndrome has contributed, in part, to the rise in the incidence of many newer disabilities and classifications, like Attention Deficit Disorder (ADD) and Attention Deficit Hyperactivity Disorder (ADHD). It also has given rise to a significant increase in medications being prescribed to school-age children. Medications such as Ritalin have exploded on the scene over the past 10 - 15 years.

This is not to say that these and other types of disorders do not exist. Rather, there is societal awareness that children potentially have these problems, and this has changed the way parents *look* at their own children. Many jump much too quickly to the conclusion that their child has an attentional or processing-based disorder before obtaining the appropriate medical and diagnostic evaluations. Some physicians also use medication on a trial and error basis to determine if it could help a child in school, rather than pursuing a more thorough diagnostic evaluation.

Parents who suspect that their child has an attentional or hyperactivity disorder should read Thomas Armstrong's book, *The Myth of the ADD Child.* Even if there is disagreement with his conclusions, it causes you to think deeply. Like the writings of Alfie Kohn, Thomas Armstrong presents arguments that challenge the traditionally held beliefs of our society.

Many professionals feel that an increasingly anxious and nervous society may be causing us to over-diagnose and overmedicate our children (See Appendix A for medications). I often joke that we are living in a society where all the teachers are on Prozac, and all the students are on Ritalin! It is said that embedded in every joke is some kernel of truth.

Blame the School Syndrome

The Blame the School Syndrome also can be explained by two patterns of parental behavior. Either the teacher (school) is incompetent and/or insensitive, or the teacher is overly demanding. Parents of children who are not performing well in school and on tests may choose the teacher or the school, rather than their child, as the target of their concern.

Certainly we all, as former students, have had enough experience to know that there are a number of less competent administrators and teachers in our school. When I think back on my schooling, I am amazed that I did so well. You know the saying, "I learned not because of my teachers but in spite of my teachers."

It is important to recognize how quickly we, as parents, make judgements about our child's teacher. If the teacher tells us that our child is very capable, but must study harder, is she right? If the teacher tells us that she thinks our child may have a language processing problem and should seek help, is she right? So much depends on trust.

If we value the teacher (school), then we are more likely to listen to what he/she says about our child.

Parents form their perceptions of teachers from comments of others and what their children report, as well as from their own observations.

There are four attributes that I believe parents should look for in their children's teachers and schools. I call them the Four C's:

Caring	A school and classroom environment that is warm, nurturing and respectful.
Compassion	An educational environment that is sensitive, empathic and compassionate to the unique needs of children and their families.
Competence	A teacher and school staff that are trained, skilled and well equipped to address the academic and social emotional needs of children.
Communication	A teacher and school that provide effective ongoing communication about children's progress and needs.

If any of these four attributes is weak or missing, the relationship between the parents and the school staff will suffer. It's all about trust!

The second pattern under Blame the School Syndrome is when parents feel that the school or teacher is overly demanding, placing too much pressure on the student to perform. Few people want a kindergarten class to be taught like a college course. It is the increasing demands for higher standards and achievement that has made this pattern of parental behavior more prevalent.

As Alfie Kohn has stated, the overemphasis on achievement has turned some of our schools into diploma factories where the primary objective is not deep learning, but high test scores. I know that his critics would argue that if the test is well developed, placing a premium on problem-solving and high level thinking skills, then the resulting scores are a reflection of deep thinking and quality learning.

The problem is that mass produced, norm-referenced, standardized tests—even the best ones—rarely measure quality. They are only one small piece of a bigger, more complex teaching and learning process. So parents who feel that their third grader is spending too much time on homework rather than playing after school may be right. Even high school students need to have time to have fun and enjoy a social life.

Many of our high powered secondary schools have really become junior colleges. High school teachers are more like professors, and the academic demands have placed great stress on our adolescents. No wonder that I meet with so many parents of adolescents who tell me that high school is stressing out their children and them. This is especially true if their child has a learning, attentional, organizational, or processing problem.

Elementary and middle schools seem better prepared to handle these types of challenges. In elementary schools, there is one primary teacher who supports the 20-25 students in his/her class. At middle school you usually have a team approach—where, although departmentalized, there is a small number of teachers who get to know the students on their team very well. At high school, however, students are expected to be more independent and responsible for their own learning. Environments are generally larger, less nurturing and less tolerant than at younger levels. High schools want to prepare kids for college, so the push is on to set expectations high.

The difference between "high" and "unrealistic" expectations tends to be at the center of the concern for many parents. Why can't the teacher adjust the curriculum, slow the pace, give students more time on assignments and homework? The answers have a lot to do with the need to prepare the students for the high stakes tests.

State education departments know that the best way to control what is taught in schools is by controlling what gets tested. Teachers will teach to the test, and if you want the bar raised, make the tests more rigorous. So parents who blame the school for being overly demanding need to recognize that many of the teachers are only doing what the state education departments are requiring of them.

On the other hand, some parents also live vicariously through their children. They want their children to be smart, successful and accomplished in life. So, if high test scores are a means to that end, they are important. This is especially true as students get older. A school district that is greatly influenced by a PTA or Board of Education that wants high test scores at almost any expense will hire administrators and teachers who will increase academic demands and keep the pressure on students.

These parents know the game and want their children to win. One way to win is to do well on tests. This explains why so many private test prep and learning centers have thrived during the last 5 to 10 years, and why tutoring has become such a great source of income for so many high school teachers. But the problem is not parents wanting the best for their children and paying for them to receive extra help. The problem is the level and intensity of parental pressure and how that may translate into a school system becoming overly demanding. As is often the case, it is the *degree* that matters.

Parenting Types

Edmund Bourne, in his best selling book, *The Anxiety and Phobia Workbook,* talks about four types of personalities which he calls "sub-personality types:"

The Worrier
The Critic
The Victim
The Perfectionist

These types were based on the earlier work of Reid Wilson and were not identified to describe parents or parenting styles. Nevertheless, I believe that they are helpful in understanding the types of parents that are most likely to promote anxiety in their children. Therefore, they have been modified to relate directly to test anxiety. Let's examine each more carefully, and explore the impact on a child's emotional development.

The Worrier

The Worrier promotes anxiety by imagining the worst. All thinking is based on the *worst case* scenario. Images of catastrophe and disaster quickly come to mind when confronted with a fearful or threatening situation. Later in Chapter 6, you will see how negative self-talk causes The Worrier to use terms like "What if..."

"What if my child doesn't study enough for the test?"
"What if he doesn't get enough sleep the night before?"

"What if my child gets sick and misses the test?"
"What if my child fails the test?"

It is quite understandable that The Worrier's child will be especially prone to anxiety and worry.

Edmund Bourne describes the three dominant tendencies in The Worrier as:

- anticipating the worst
- overestimating the odds of something bad or embarrassing happening
- creating grandiose images of potential failure or catastrophe

Imagine a parent who was just informed that his/her child will be taking a high stakes test later in the school year. Think of the types of behavior that The Worrier might exhibit:

- calling the school to find out as much about the test as possible ("When it will be given?" "How will they prepare the kids?" "Who will score it?" etc.)
- asking the teacher detailed questions about the test itself ("How long is it?" "Is it timed?" "How many items?" etc.)
- talking to parents of older children to find out about their child's experiences on the test ("How well did they do?" "Did they find it to be a hard test?" etc.)
- talking to their child about the importance of studying and doing well on the test
- finding a tutor or test prep center for their child to attend after school
- going to the bookstore to find copies of past tests so their child can practice

- surfing the Internet for information.

On the surface, none of these behaviors seem inappropriate. But, if I tell you that this high stakes test is being given at the end of third grade, your concerns about this parent's actions might be somewhat different. As I said earlier, it is the *degree* that matters.

The Worrier not only promotes anxiety, but can contribute to the development of psychiatric conditions like Obsessive Compulsive Disorder (OCD) in his or her child. Some amount of worry and anticipatory concern can help prepare and mobilize us; however, too much worry may become pathological. Remember, we want *optimal* levels of test anxiety, not hysteria!

The Critic

This type describes the parent who is highly judge-mental of his/her child. Often characterized as the overly-critical parent who draws attention to a child's limitations, weaknesses or flaws, The Critic uses sarcasm and putdowns. Kids coming from homes where one or both parents are critics tend to have low self-esteem because these types of parents focus on mistakes and constantly compare them to others who are more successful. Critical parents use state-ments like:

"You could have done better."
"What's wrong with you?"
"Can't you ever get it right?"
"You are a disappointment."
"You will never amount to anything."

Three major tendencies of The Critic are:

- being highly judgemental and opinionated

- ignoring the positives and focuses on the negatives
- comparing his/her child to others (usually in a negative way)

Unless they are naturally very good at test-taking, children who live with The Critic are likely to be test-anxious. They know that there is very little margin for error. If they do poorly, they will not only disappoint their parent, but may suffer much verbal criticism, perhaps even punishment.

The Victim

This type of parent promotes feelings of helplessness or hopelessness. These parents can be effective enablers because they tell their children that they are not responsible for their condition or performance. They are classic Blame the Child believers. They believe that conditions such as being poor, having a disability, experiencing emotional problems or other unfortunate life events have made their children unable to perform well. They see themselves and their children as victims of circumstances beyond their control.

Therefore, these parents want the school to cater to and/or expect less from their children. They feel that they have been dealt a "bad hand." And now, society and others owe it to them to make it up. They often feel that their child is entitled to special treatment. And if they don't get what they want, Victim parents can then easily shift to the Blame the School syndrome behavior. "How insensitive this school is for not meeting the special needs of my helpless child."

The Victim-type parents can also feel very depressed about their condition and have very low expectations for their children. Statements about children associated with The Victim include:

"They can't do that."

"They will never be able to do that."

"Can't they be exempted from taking the test?"

Three major tendencies of The Victim are:

- enabling through promoting helplessness
- setting very low expectations for the child
- promoting feelings of dependence

Unfortunately we are living in a society where more and more parents are viewing their children and themselves as victims.

The Perfectionist

Of the four parenting types, The Perfectionist is, perhaps, the one most closely associated with test anxiety. This may be due to the fact that the push by society toward higher achievement, more rigorous standards, and advanced degrees has nurtured a fertile environment in which The Perfectionist can thrive.

The Perfectionist is related to The Critic, but he/she is less inclined to put the child down, and more concerned with driving the child to be the *best*. This type of parent instills in the child that self-worth is determined through extrinsic success—such as achievement, money, job status, and acceptance by others.

Unfortunately, this type of parent does not nurture a child's intrinsic feelings of self-worth. Instead, he or she suggests that everything important in life is based upon what others think and feel.

The Perfectionist is a driven individual who constantly generates anxiety because things are never quite good enough. Everything for the perfectionist is centered around "shoulds."

"You should have done better."
"You should be working harder.
"You should always do well in school."
"You should have aced the test.

The tendencies of The Perfectionist are:

- wanting everything to be perfect

- wanting everything under control

- focusing on competition and being driven by the child being the best

- viewing self-worth as externally derived

Imagine the impact of increased testing in the home of The Perfectionist, especially if the child is not a good test- taker.

There are many other parent personality types and styles that we could discuss. However, our goal should not be to label parents, but to recognize that their behaviors can have a significant impact on their children's anxieties about school, tests, and life. Furthermore, there can be many different combinations of these personality types. The mother who is The Worrier and the father who is The Critic. Or the father who is The Perfectionist and the mother who is The Victim.

Chapters 5, 6, and 7 will provide some useful strate-gies to more effectively reduce test anxiety generated by these parent types and their child-rearing practices. We must not underestimate the role that child rearing plays in the development of childhood and adolescent anxiety. With the increase in high stakes testing, parents now have even more opportunities to influence their children's approach to school and its many challenges. Whether test anxiety be-comes a major problem may greatly depend on what begins in the home.

Chart VI

Four Parent Personality Types That Promote Anxiety

Type	Characteristics	Statements
The Worrier	• anticipates the worst • overestimates the odds of bad things happening • creates images of failure and catastrophe	"What if..."
The Critic	• highly judgemental • ignores positive and focuses on the negative • compares child to others	"You could have..."
The Victim	• enables through helplessness • sets low expectations • promotes feelings of dependence	"You can't..."
The Perfectionist	• wants everything perfect and under control • focuses on competition • views self-worth as externally derived	"You should have..."

And Teachers (as Stakeholders)...

Why do so many teachers contribute to high levels of test anxiety? After all, they want their students to perform well. They should know better than anyone that high stress levels in their students are counterproductive to good test scores.

The answer is, teachers have to survive in school cultures where standardized testing is becoming an increasingly important part of life. They, too, must "play the game." "Leave no child behind...we must test everyone" has become the new motto. Most educators, teachers and administrators alike know that state and local testing is getting out of hand. But it is not *politically correct* for an educator to express such an opinion.

But, how can teachers be held responsible if there are no objective standardized tests? How will we know *what* kids are learning or *if* they are learning unless we test them? There appears to be no other way to hold schools and teachers accountable except through a well structured testing program. Or at least, that is what the establishment says.

The fact that there are other means of assessment, such as portfolios, projects, student exhibitions and performances just doesn't cut it. State education departments want assessments that are "teacher proof," assessments that remove, as much as possible, teacher judgment. Objective tests that can be easily scored and minimize any subjectivity are most popular. Tests then can be used to compare large groups of students to others.

To address the criticism that these types of tests often generate, state education departments are beginning to include some small essay-type questions that need to be scored by teachers using state developed rubrics. A rubric is a means to assess work and performances utilizing agreed upon criteria with clear gradations of quality identified.

However, the increasing amount of time needed to release teachers from classrooms to score these items, as well as concerns about inter-rater reliability, are making this process very cumbersome to manage and difficult to monitor on a statewide basis. State education departments should be commended for any efforts to broaden the way students are assessed. Educators know that children learn in many different ways, so they should be assessed in many different ways.

Chart VII

Types of Assessments

More Objective	More Subjective
Standardized, norm-referenced tests	Portfolios
Machine scorable tests	Student performances & exhibitions
Multiple choice tests	Projects & written essays
Matching & short answer, fact-based tests	Authentic assessments

---

Motivational Factors

I believe that teachers have great influence over the test anxiety felt by children. Many years ago I was trained by one of the foremost educators of the late 20th century, Madeline Hunter. She believed that students' motivation to learn could be influenced by the teacher using a concept she called "level of concern." Namely, if a teacher raised or lowered a student's level of concern, the teacher could ensure that the motivation to learn was set at the right level. One way to raise the level of concern is to make kids accountable for what they have learned. What I didn't realize at the time was that Madeline Hunter's concept of level of concern is in some ways analogous to the anxiety levels explained in Chapter 2. If I wanted to raise students' level of concern, I might tell them that I am going to call on them tomorrow in class and ask them to share what they had just learned. If I wanted to lower highly anxious students' level of concern I might say "Read this story tonight, but I am not going to quiz you on it tomorrow."

Like anxiety, if a student's level of concern was too low, he or she would not be interested in learning and/or retaining the content that was taught. In turn, if the student's level of concern was too high, the student might not be able to concentrate on the teaching or might become too anxious to retrieve it at a later time—like for a test.

Level of concern was only one of a total of six factors that Madeline Hunter identified as having a powerful effect on motivation. Each of these factors can be greatly influenced by the behaviors of the teacher. They presume, however, that the teacher knows his/her students well. The following chart provides a brief overview and description of each of the six motivational factors.

Chart VIII

Madeline Hunter's Motivational Factors

Level of Concern — The extent to which the learner cares about the learning. Not caring is equivalent to not trying. Caring too much can lead to fear of trying.

Feeling Tone — The pleasantness or unpleasantness of the learning situation. Feeling tones exist on a continuum which teachers create through their words and actions.

Success — Learners' feelings of success are related to accomplishment. The level of difficulty of the task must be set at the proper level of challenge.

Interest — Interest is not innate, it is acquired. A teacher can relate material to the learners' interests or make material more interesting through the use of novelty.

Knowledge of Results — The amount, specificity, and immediacy of feedback that the learner receives.

Intrinsic-Extrinsic Motivation — Both are effective and teachers need to understand how extrinsic motivation can lead to intrinsic motivation.

Madeline Hunter's work focused primarily on the teacher's role in the teaching and learning process. It was not until years later that research began focusing more on how kids learn than how teachers teach. But for our purposes, the role of teachers in raising and/or lowering the levels of test anxiety felt by their students is critical. In order to do this effectively, teachers must know their students well enough to identify those who are at risk for test anxiety, and differentiate the strategies needed to help these students manage their test anxiety.

Beginning to Assess

How can teachers best begin to find out how their students are feeling? The answer can be explained by the following story:

> Jamal, a poor, inner city five-year-old African American boy, had just been adopted by a white couple living in an affluent, predominantly white, upper middle class community.

> Everything about Jamal's adjustment to his new life in the suburbs seemed fine. He made friends in his neighborhood and appeared to be a happy and well-adjusted young boy given all the changes that he had recently experienced in his life.

> Shortly after entering Kindergarten, his teacher noted that all of Jamal's artwork was being drawn with black and brown colors.

> She collected his artwork over several weeks and showed it to the principal, who in turn gave the artwork to the school psychologist for his assessment.

Given Jamal's situation, there certainly were enough issues that could be brewing below the surface. After all, he was only one of two African American students in a 600 pupil elementary school. He had just been adopted and relocated to a dramatically different living environment. If anyone could have unresolved issues that could manifest through artwork, it was Jamal.

But the psychologist was a wise professional. Instead of giving Jamal a series of projective tests to assess what was going on, he decided to observe Jamal in art class.

So one day, the psychologist sat down next to Jamal, who was seated at the end of a long series of tables in the art room. Jamal was drawing a picture of a boat based on a story that his teacher had read to his class earlier in the day. By the way, he was using black and brown crayons to draw.

Right next to Jamal on the table was a nearly empty large metal container with several other black and brown crayons lying at the bottom.

The psychologist brought a number of Jamal's drawings that the teacher and principal had shared with him. He showed each to Jamal and asked him, "Why do you use only black and brown colors to draw with?"

Jamal paused and pointed down the long expanse of tables and said to the psychologist, "By the time the crayons get to me, those are the only colors left!"

What a great story! Teachers may not need to psy-choanalyze their test-anxious students. Psychologists may not need to take out their Rorschach inkblots. What they need to do first is to talk to kids. Ask them questions. Try and find out how they are feeling. Keep it simple.

Instead of putting Jamal in therapy, the art teacher needed more red, green, blue, and yellow crayons. Instead of first setting up therapy groups on test anxiety, begin by asking some basic questions.

Of course, if Jamal later develops delayed adjustment problems that could be resolved through counseling, it should be implemented. And if some of a teacher's test-anxious students are literally phobic about the testing situation, then more intensive help needs to be given. But schools should not start with the assumption of the worst case scenario.

Once students at risk for test anxiety are identified, then teachers need to differentiate specific strategies to help them address their various learning problems. A number of specific techniques and strategies that teachers can implement are presented in Chapters 5, 6 and 7.

And Kids (as Stakeholders)...Oh, my!

Some of the worries that kids have about school are quite normal. New and unknown experiences can trigger anxious feelings and these typical anxieties are a normal part of life—like the first day of a new school year. Similarly, there are typical worries which are a normal part of any new and/or important assessment experience. It is normal to have some worry about taking the SATs or ACTs. But kids need to learn to keep those worries under control and not allow them to develop into a high state of anxiety.

Chart IX

Typical Test-Taking Worries

Issue	Anxiety
Location/Time	Where is the test being given and at what time? (And, how early should I get there?)
Preparation	What will be on the test? What should I study?
Materials	What do I need to bring?
Results	When will I get my results?

In addition to parents and teachers, kids themselves can raise their own test anxiety levels. There are at least three ways that kids contribute to their own levels of test anxiety:

- **Sharing feelings**
- **Peer pressure**
- **Self-perception**

Each can have a positive or negative impact on anxiety.

Sharing Feelings

The first way that kids may contribute to each other's high levels of anxiety is when they communicate to one another how they feel about a test. For example:

John says to Susie: "I am really worried about tomorrow's test, aren't you?"

Billy says to Laura: "I took that test last year. I wasted my time studying. It was just too hard."

Rick says to Owen: "You know if you fail that math test, you will be put in a lower level in high school."

Julie says to Brad: "My counselor told me that if we don't score at least 1200 on the SAT we can forget about applying to ____(college)____."

Kids talking to kids, especially in the middle, high school and college years, can be a source of great anxiety. If students know that comments by others can heighten their anxiety, then they should not talk too much with others. It is like the kid who is anxious about going on the new inverted rollercoaster. That kid should not stand near the exit and listen to those getting off talking about how scary it was.

Now, this communication can cut both ways. Kids can help other kids lower their feelings of anxiety as well, and form a more positive frame of mind. For example:

Chris says to Josh: "We have been really studying for next week's test. I feel that we are prepared and will do well."

Katie says to Ann: "I talked to my brother who took the test last year. He said it is not as hard as we think."

Mark says to Kim: "It's OK. If we don't do well on this test, we can take it again in August."

Leigh says to Ally: "I know our combined SAT score is important, but it is not the only thing colleges will be looking at."

The message from one peer to another does not, in and of itself, inherently carry a positive or negative message. Three factors contribute to a message being interpreted as positive or negative in terms of reducing high levels of anxiety:

- The message itself - Does the message convey a feeling that is positive, supportive and anxiety-reducing or not?

- The relationship with the peer - the degree to which one values the peer's perspective or opinion on a topic. Namely, if it is felt that a peer is not knowledgable or trustworthy about an issue being discussed, then the comments are likely to be dismissed.

- The interpretation of the message - the peer's intention may be to reduce anxiety and be positive, but the message's interpretation could actually have the opposite effect.

For example, let's more closely examine one of the peer statements listed above.

Mark says to Kim: "It's OK, if we don't do well on this test we can take it again in August."

What Mark is *really* saying: "If we do poorly, we can study again and do better next time. This is not a 'do or die' situation."

Sounds as if Mark's intention is to be supportive by taking the pressure off. Namely, "we have another chance, so let's not freak out."

Kim's interpretation could be:

#1 "Great. I feel better—because I know I will have another chance to pass the test."

#2 "What does Mark know, he always fails tests."

#3 "This is terrible. I've got to pass it now— because I am going on a family vacation in August."

The interpretation #3 actually increased the pressure on Kim. She now worries that if she fails the test the first time, she will be interfering with her family's vacation in August. Mark probably had no knowledge or information about Kim's family plans.

To more effectively address the impact of statements made by peers, kids need to recognize what they are really saying to themselves. Positive self-talk, a technique that addresses this issue, is covered later in Chapter 6.

Peer Pressure

We all know the power of peer pressure. The problem is that it is very difficult for adults to influence it. As parents know, trying to control who are the friends your child hangs out with is something like controlling the weather. So, kids must learn how to handle peer pressure for themselves. For example:

Jen says to Patty: "Several of us are going to study after school. You had better join us if you want to do well on the test."

| David and Charlie say to Andrew: | "Only nerds study for this type of test. You aren't a nerd, are you Andrew?" |

Peer pressure is very complex to analyze since it is also related to an individual's feeling of self-worth. The more that individuals are insecure about themselves and feel that the opinions of others are important, the more they succumb to peer pressure. Children raised in the homes of parents that fit the profile of The Critic or The Perfectionist are more apt to be affected by peer pressure. Once again, as with kids sharing their feelings, peer pressure can play a positive or negative role in test anxiety.

Self-Perception

Kids begin to distinguish what they are *good* at from what they are *not good* at very early in their school experience. They think things like, "I'm a good speller," "I'm a good reader," "I'm a terrible writer," "I stink at math." Often they distinguish between these two categories (*good* and *not good*) by identifying what comes easy to them in school from what doesn't. "I am not good at math because it takes me a long time to figure out the right answers." This perception then translates into: "I know I am just going to do terribly on tomorrow's math test. After all, it's timed."

And guess what? The student does poorly on the math test. This is an example of a self-induced fear based on a self-perception that actually contributes to poor performance. It is the worst type of self-fulfilling prophecy.

Self-perception really functions at two levels:

- **In the mirror**
- **On the stage**

In the mirror refers to how kids view themselves through their own self-evaluation. Kids are often their own worst critic, and as such, are often harder on themselves than others would be. This image is formed over many years as a result of many influences from their parents, to the experiences of school, their teachers and classmates. It reflects their true inner beliefs and feelings about their strengths and weaknesses, and does not change easily.

On the stage refers to the self-perceptions that kids want others to see. It is the extent to which they reveal or do not reveal themselves to others. In other words, do they want others to know about their self-perception? For example, the child who is anxious about a test but doesn't want anyone to know it may try to appear outwardly calm or cool.

If what children reveal about their inner feelings to peers, family and friends, is not consistent with their "in the mirror" self-perception, then they are exerting much energy. It is difficult to maintain a "front." Furthermore, anxiety is likely to increase because they actually begin to worry that others may find out the *truth* about their self-perception.

In summary, kids' contributions to their own test anxiety occurs in three ways: sharing feelings, peer pressure, and self-perception. Each of these can have a positive result, thus reducing anxiety, or a negative result which can increase anxiety. Ultimately, the technique of positive self-talk, explained in Chapter 6, will help students more effectively deal with all three of these factors.

The age and maturity of the kid may have either a positive or negative impact. If kids attempt to better know themselves and their emotions, they will be better equipped to control their test anxiety. As we will see in Chapter 4, Emotional Intelligence may be more important than IQ!

Chart X

Kids' Contribution to Test Anxiety
(Examples)

	Positive Result (Reduces Anxiety)	Negative Result (Increases Anxiety)
Sharing Feelings	Reassurance and reduction of feeling alone	Increased anxiety and feelings of isolation
Peer Pressure	Increased time spent studying for test	Decreased likelihood of studying for test
Self-Perception	Increased motivation to prepare	Decreased motivation to prepare

Like the characters in *The Wizard of Oz*, these three stakeholder groups (the parents, the teachers, and the kids) need to find the *heart, brain,* but especially the *courage* to address the many challenges of test anxiety.

Chapter 4
Controlling Test Anxiety:
A Framework for Understanding

How do we go about addressing and ultimately controlling the level of test anxiety in our children? First we
need to approach it within a logical framework that includes
three phases:

- **Pre-Testing Phase**
- **Test-in-Progress Phase**
- **Post-Testing Phase**

Let us examine each of these phases and recognize the
important roles that the stakeholder groups (parents, teachers and kids) can play in controlling the level of test anxiety
at each phase.

Second, we will explore an important theory in each
phase that furthers our understanding about instructional
preparation, the roles of emotions and the choices we make
related to test anxiety.

Third, a model that greatly helps us untangle the
multiple layers of symptoms that contribute to test anxiety is
presented. This information and theoretical foundation

provides the context for the strategies and techniques covered in Chapters 5, 6, and 7. Understanding and ultimately controlling test anxiety is very complex, and we cannot get at the heart of it unless we break it down into its component parts.

Pre-Testing Phase

Pre-testing is the longest of the three phases, since its beginning is marked at the time a test is first announced and concludes when the test is administered. Although parents can and do play a major role during the pre-testing phase, it is the teacher who has the largest role. The way a teacher announces and prepares the students for the test, as well as the messages conveyed during the pre-testing phase, are all critical to raising and/or lowering test anxiety.

During the pre-testing phase it is best to use resources that are targeted at preparing students for the test. The more prepared students are, the more confident and less anxious they will feel.

In this phase, teachers have four primary responsibilities. These include:

- communicating effectively about the upcoming test
- finding ways to increase students' understanding of the necessary content
- helping teach and promote effective study skills and habits
- using examples and practice tests to help students prepare.

Although a number of valuable strategies and techniques are presented in the next chapter to address each of these goals, performing well on tests ultimately begins with an effective teaching and learning environment.

This book is focused on reducing the debilitating effects of high test anxiety. But it makes an important assumption. Namely, that the teacher has created a positive and differentiated learning environment. Effective preparation of students cannot occur unless their diverse learning styles and intelligences are accounted for.

Differentiated Instruction

Research demonstrates that to meet the diverse learning needs of today's children, teachers must use differentiated instructional practices—practices that more effectively enable teachers to reach and teach all students. Carol Ann Tomlinson, author of *How to Differentiate Instruction in Mixed Ability Classrooms*, identifies effective differentiated instruction as having several characteristics.

When differentiated instruction is proactive, teachers plan instruction in order to address the wide range of diverse learners in their classrooms. The multiplicity of needs are acknowledged initially and included from the initial stages of planning.

Making differentiated instruction more qualitative than quantitative requires the teacher to think deeply about the teaching process. It is not adequate to solely look at the amount of work required; it is also necessary to look at the breath and depth of concepts.

Incorporating continuous assessment is a critical element of differentiation as it not only provides students with an appreciation of where they are in the learning process, but enables the teacher to implement instruction in ways that help students make the most of their potentials and talents.

Tomlinson also identifies the need for multiple approaches to what students learn and how they learn, as well as ways they demonstrate that learning. A student-centered element adds a focus on what students bring to the teaching-learning environment.

Providing a combination of settings for learning is also seen as critical; this recognizes that a teacher needs to be skilled in providing instruction to the entire class but also must be able to use grouping effectively, and know when individual instruction is warranted.

The last characteristic relates to the need for teachers to be reflective, and amenable to changing and refining their instruction. This is referred to as an "organic" component to differentiated instruction.

If every teacher understood the importance and value of differentiated instruction, preparation for tests would be markedly improved. Students would be more effectively reached and multiple pathways would be utilized by teachers to help students better understand content, as well as demonstrate what they have learned. The more secure students are in their knowledge of content, the less anxious they will be at test time. In this way, effective classroom instruction and test anxiety are integrally linked.

Carol Ann Tomlinson, Diane Heacox, as well as Gayle Gregory and Carolyn Chapman, have written widely on this topic of differentiated instruction. I encourage all teachers to read more about this approach and implement this "way of life" in their classrooms.

In addition to differentiated instruction, one of the most powerful understandings that teachers (and parents) must have in meeting the needs of diverse learners is the use of Multiple Intelligences theory.

Multiple Intelligences (MI)

Dr. Howard Gardner is a professor at Harvard University, and an author of numerous books, such as *Frames of Mind, Multiple Intelligences, The Unschooled Mind,* and *The Disciplined Mind.* He is also a senior co-director of Project Zero, a research group at Harvard's Graduate School of Education that explores the development of learning in children, adults and organizations. It was through Howard Gardner's groundbreaking work nearly 20 years ago that society began to view intelligence as having multiple domains.

Multiple Intelligences (MI) is a psychological theory that has had a profound impact on the field of education, causing educators to rethink what it means to be smart. No longer do we ask "How smart are our kids?", but "How are our kids smart?" Gardner defines intelligence as an ability to use a skill, make a product or solve a problem that is valued by a particular culture.

Contrary to most traditional views of intelligence, MI argues that individuals can be intelligent across a wide variety of domains. Gardner categorized those types of skills and abilities that seem to be common across all human beings regardless of time and culture. Thus, intelligences are seen as potentials that are nurtured at a very early age in children. Individuals may have greater potentials in some domains than in others, but each is capable of achieving his or her potential in the various intelligence domains.

Gardner views intelligences as bio-psychological potentials. In other words, we adapt to the world by possessing various skills and abilities that enable us to interact effectively with the environment. Each of us has a unique combination of these potentials. MI provides a framework to help teachers identify ways to differentiate their assessments, instruction and student work. It also has great implications for assessment.

The Original Seven

Intelligence has traditionally been viewed as a single, general capacity that can be measured in all individuals, usually by a standardized verbal and/or written test. Gardner, on the other hand, identified at least seven intelligences. These include:

• **Linguistic Intelligence** – An individual's capacity to use language effectively as a means of expression and communication. (Examples of careers or end states: poets, writers.)

• **Logical/Mathematical Intelligence** – An individual's capacity to think logically, use numbers effectively, solve problems scientifically, and figure out relationships and patterns between concepts and things. (Examples of careers or end states: mathematicians, scientists.)

• **Spatial Intelligence** – An individual's capacity to think visually and orient oneself spatially. In addition, spatially intelligent people are able to graphically represent their visual and spatial ideas. (Examples of careers or end states: artists, decorators, architects, surveyors, inventors, guides.)

• **Musical Intelligence** – The capacity to appreciate a variety of musical forms in addition to using music as a vehicle of expression. Musically intelligent people are sensitive to rhythm, melody, and pitch. (Examples of careers or end states: singers, musicians, composers.)

• **Bodily Kinesthetic Intelligence** – The capacity to use one's own body skillfully as a means of expression, or to work skillfully to create or manipulate objects. (Examples of careers or end states: dancers, actors, athletes, sculptors, surgeons, mechanics, craftspeople.)

• **Interpersonal Intelligence** – The capacity to appropriately and effectively respond to other people and understand their feelings. (Examples of careers or end states: sales people, social directors, travel agents, politicians.)

• **Intrapersonal Intelligence** – The capacity to accurately know one's self, including knowledge of one's own strengths, motivations, goals, and feelings. (Examples of careers or end states: entrepreneurs, therapists.)

Interpersonal Intelligence and Intrapersonal Intelligence are also referred to as personal intelligences. These intelligences remain among the most controversial and directly relate to a new body of research know as Emotional Intelligence discussed later in this chapter.

Newer Intelligences

Since Gardner identified the original seven intelligences, two more have been added:

• **Naturalist Intelligence** – The ability to understand, relate to, categorize, classify, comprehend, and explain the things encountered in the world of nature. (Examples of careers or end states: farmers, ranchers, hunters, gardeners, animal handlers.)

• **Existential Intelligence*** – Gardner believes that some individuals may possess the ability to deal with questions concerning the meaning of life, e.g. spirituality, metaphysical speculations. (Examples of careers or end states: philosophers, religious leaders, poets.)

---

* Not yet officially identified as an intelligence

Chart XI

Howard Gardner's Multiple Intelligences (MI)

Intelligences	Kinds of Smart
Linguistic	Word Smart
Logical/Mathematical	Math Smart
Musical	Music Smart
Spatial	Picture Smart
Bodily/Kinesthetic	Body Smart
Interpersonal	People Smart
Intrapersonal	Self Smart
Naturalist Intelligence	Nature Smart

Sometimes referred to as 8 ½ intelligences, the number is not what is important. Whether there are eight or twenty-eight is not the issue. What is important is that intelligence should not be viewed as a single entity, but as multiple potentials that extend across many domains. We must recognize that students learn in many different ways, and that there are multiple entry points to their learning. Therefore, we must teach and assess students in many different ways. The impact of Multiple Intelligence theory on the way we teach in our schools, and ultimately on the way we assess our children, is profound.

Historically, the types of intelligences most closely associated with schools and testing were linguistic and logical/mathematical intelligences – the ability to work with words and numbers, respectively. Thomas Armstrong later referred to children possessing high levels of these two types of intelligences as being *word smart* and *number smart*.

However, MI theory identifies a wide range of different intelligences that cannot be adequately measured with paper and pencil tests. These intelligences are equally as important as linguistic and logical/mathematical, and are arguably even more important to success in life.

Project Spectrum, supported by Harvard's Project Zero and Tuft's University and funded by the Spencer Foundation, was an effort to identify distinctive intellectual strengths in young children. This ten-year research project was dedicated to developing an alternative approach to curriculum and assessment – an approach like that of Montessori and others that respects the diverse interests and abilities that children bring to preschool and early childhood environments. Project Spectrum emphasized a less prescriptive use of materials with the teacher's role being less regulated in regards to the use of those materials and the workspace. Project Spectrum provided a framework for multiple assessment of cognitive abilities in context while offering multiple entry points into the curriculum. It did not tell teachers or schools what they should teach, but certainly emphasized the fact that there had to be multiple pathways to both learning and to assessment.

Test-in-Progress Phase

This phase begins just before the test is given, continues through the administration, and ends when the test is completed. It is this period of time when the symptoms of test anxiety are most strongly felt. It could extend from a day or two before the test until the test booklet is closed and handed in.

In this phase, the student is like a soldier who knows

that he's going into battle. The intensity of his anxiety rises as the date and time draw near. Once in the battle, emotions peak and the soldier's success largely depends on his preparation and on his physical, emotional, and mental ability to withstand the pressures of war. Will he live to fight another day or will he become overcome by his emotions?

Similarly, the student facing a high stakes test may be anxious. The intensity increases as the date and time of the test draw near. All the content preparation in the world will be rendered useless if the student's anxiety is too high. The student will panic and not be able to concentrate or retrieve necessary information. Will he live to be tested another day or will he freak out?

We must prepare students not only academically, but emotionally for these high stakes tests. This is done by addressing the physical, emotional, and mental/cognitive symptoms of test anxiety head on. In Chapter 6, specific strategies and techniques to lower high anxiety and stress levels in the heat of battle are discussed.

Since students must call upon and use these techniques when anxious, I've chosen to list them in the test-in-progress phase. In this phase, the student is in control, no longer the teacher (or the parent for that matter). It's mano-on-mano—you and the test. Who will be the victor in this battle depends on the success of the preparation in the pre-testing phase, and the success of the anxiety reducing techniques employed in the test-in-progress phase.

Emotional Intelligence (EI)

Peter Salovey, professor of psychology at Yale University, to whom I am deeply indebted, is the co-developer of one of the most useful theories to help us explain and understand intelligence. This theory has generated considerable research over the past 12 years and is critical to our understanding of test anxiety.

Emotional Intelligence is a theory that builds on Gardner's personal intelligences and extends our traditional view of what it means to be smart. Emotional Intelligence was first proposed in 1990 by Salovey and his colleague, John D. Mayer of the University of New Hampshire. Daniel Goleman popularized their ideas in his internationally best-selling book, *Emotional Intelligence: Why it Can Matter More than IQ*, published in 1995.

In its broadest sense, intelligence can be defined as the ability to adapt successfully to one's environment. It is argued that emotional intelligence may be more important than IQ because success in personal relationships and in the workplace may be more dependent on how we manage and regulate our emotions than on our cognitive abilities. Emotions can be used to motivate ourselves and can help us adapt more efficiently to our environment. Although research on emotional intelligence has rapidly grown, there is still much to be learned. Salovey and Mayer identify intelligence along four branches:

- **Identifying and expressing emotions** – the capacity to perceive and to express feelings.

- **Understanding emotions and emotional knowledge** – the ability to label emotions, to understand complex emotions, and to know the likely transitions between emotions.

- **Using emotions** – the use of emotions to facilitate cognitive processes, such as reasoning, creativity and problem solving.

- **Managing emotions** – the ability to regulate emotions in oneself and in other people.

In *Emotional Intelligence*, Daniel Goleman varies from Salovey and Mayer's original formulation and describes five abilities that comprise emotional intelligence:

- **Knowing one's emotion** – the ability to recognize and interpret one's own emotional states.
- **Recognizing emotions in others** – the ability to read "emotional states" in other people.
- **Managing emotions in one's self** – the ability to regulate one's emotions.
- **Using emotions to motivate one's self** – the ability to use one's own emotions to motivate action or to guide one's thinking.
- **Handling relationships** – the ability to regulate the emotions of others.

No book on test anxiety would be complete without the understanding of the role emotions play in the way we function and communicate. No field has been more excited about the theory of Emotional Intelligence than education. Educators have embraced Emotional Intelligence because it makes so much sense. There is an increasing body of work known as emotional literacy, where emotional skills are explicitly taught to students. We all know intuitively that our emotions play a very significant role in our lives. Emotion, in and of itself, is not a hindrance to our ability to function in life, but actually is complementary to other skills such as our cognitive skills. Learning how to identify, understand, use and manage our emotions are very valuable skills.

Individuals with what is called high Emotional Intelligence, or high EQ, are individuals who can recognize differences in the emotional expressions of others, have the ability to adjust feedback and regulate their own emotions. Thus, they create environments that can be very successful, not only for themselves, but for those around them. The teacher with a high EQ is the more effective teacher. The boss in the workplace with the high EQ is the more effective leader. The student with a high EQ is less anxious when approaching difficult tasks such as high stakes testing.

Chart XII
Emotional Intelligence (EI) Models

Salovey & Mayer's Model
- Identifying & expressing emotions
- Understanding emotions
- Using emotions
- Managing emotions

Goleman's Model
- Knowing one's emotions
- Recognizing emotions in others
- Managing emotions
- Using emotions to motivate
- Handling relationships

Emotional skills play a critical role in achieving success both in school and in the "real world." The ability to regulate one's emotions in one's self and in others, the ability to handle emotional problems that arise in school, and the ability to motivate one's self to adequately prepare for a test are all examples of how emotional intelligence is important.

Emotions and the Brain

Much of the support for the theory of EI is based on neuroscientific research, particularly that of Joseph LeDoux at The Center for Neural Science at New York University. He was the first to discover the role of a small almond-shaped cluster of cells called the amygdala. It is located at the base of the temporal lobe (in the basal ganglia) near the thalamus and hypothalamus.

The amygdala is widely recognized as the emotional core of the brain that has the primary role of triggering the fear response. It also imprints in memory the most significant moments of emotional arousal. The more that the amygdala is aroused, the stronger the memory becomes. That is why we remember traumatic events so vividly—more than less traumatic experiences.

Research by Michael Davis at Emory University in Atlanta has focused on a pea-size knot of neurons located near the amygdala which is called the bed nucleus of the stria terminalis (BNST). BNST may be at the root of anxiety disorders. However more research needs to be done.

Daniel Goleman used the term *emotional hijacking* to explain how emotions can so totally overtake the brain's functioning when someone is in a rage or loses control. In the same way, high levels of test anxiety can hijack a test-taker who can literally have a panic attack and experience physiological symptoms identical to fear. Cognitive abilities are altered. The ability to concentrate and focus is lost. The ability to remember and/or retrieve information is greatly weakened.

Patricia Wolfe, author of *Brain Matters: Translating Research into Classroom Practice,* argues that teachers must match instruction to how the brain learns best. This so-called "brain-based" learning maximizes strategies that increase retention and understanding, as well as the students' abilities to apply the concepts that they are learning. A number of these type of strategies are identified later in Chapters 5 and 6.

Test Anxiety Triangle

To better explain the clusters of test anxiety symptoms that occur during the test-in-progress phase, they have been sorted into three components:

- **Physical Component**
- **Emotional Component**
- **Mental or Cognitive Component**

The three components work together in unison, and it is virtually impossible to isolate one from the other. Envision a triangle with test anxiety in the middle, and each corner being one of these three components (See Chart XIII). I call it the Test Anxiety Triangle. Like the Bermuda Triangle, once you enter it, strange things can happen!

Although test anxiety is a total mind/body reaction to a perceived threat, I will attempt to explain each of the three components. However, the separation of these components is purely artificial, and for discussion purposes only. The physical, emotional and cognitive symptoms of test anxiety are all interrelated. I will also provide specific strategies and techniques to address each component in Chapter 6. Since the physical, emotional and cognitive factors that contribute to test anxiety all work together, using techniques to alleviate the symptoms of one of the components can also positively affect the others.

△ Physical Component

Perhaps the easiest place to start is with the physical symptoms associated with test anxiety. These are the most observable, both to the individual and to others, since they involve the body's reactions to anxiety. These physical responses to test anxiety can be divided into at least seven different categories:

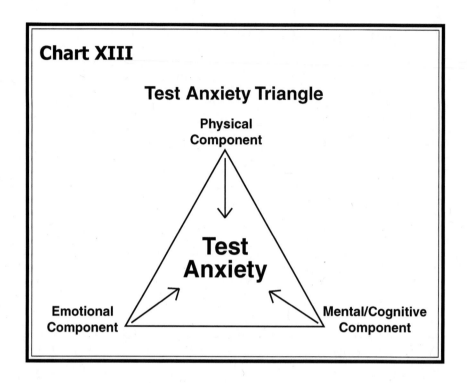

Chart XIII

Test Anxiety Triangle

Physical Component

Test Anxiety

Emotional Component

Mental/Cognitive Component

Body temperature response

One of the most common symptoms of anxiety is a noticeable and sometimes rapid change in body temperature. Often times, individuals begin to feel very warm. They perspire and their palms begin to sweat. However, body temperature can also be lower under stress. An individual may feel cold, with hands becoming "clammy".

Breathing response

Another physical symptom relates to changes in breathing. The most extreme case is hyperventilating. Breathing can be a critical factor during anxiety because of its impact on the amount of oxygen in our bodies.

Muscular response
Stiffness in areas of the body, such as the shoulders, neck and back are often reported during testing, as is shakiness, especially in the extremities. Also, weakness in the legs or knees is also commonly reported.

Abdominal response
How often have you heard someone say before a test, "I have butterflies in my stomach"? The stomach and abdominal areas are common locations of symptoms, with upset stomachs and nausea being high on the list.

Head/senses responses
Symptoms associated with the head area and the senses are also very prevalent—headaches, feeling faint, dizziness, or light-headedness are often reported. Blurred vision is also commonly experienced.

Cardiovascular responses
Most often associated with full fledged panic attacks are cardiovascular symptoms, such as palpitations and a tightness in the chest. Test anxiety can increase blood pressure and lead to the feeling of a knot in one's throat or chest.

Other physically-based responses

There is also an array of other physical symptoms associated with test anxiety. These include:

- skin rashes
- changes in eating patterns (eating too much or too little)
- an increase or decrease in activity level
- sleep disorders such as insomnia (remember my daughter, Kalyn)
- nightmares, or even in severe cases of phobia, night terrors may be present
- an increase in alcohol, tobacco or drug use.

When you consider all these symptoms and the reality that often a combination of these body responses occur during high test anxiety situations, you can readily understand why test performance suffers.

△ Emotional Component

The second primary component of the Test Anxiety Triangle addresses the emotional symptoms of anxiety. Emotional responses to test anxiety can be categorized into three areas:

- **Mood responses**
- **Emotionally labile responses**
- **Feelings of losing control**

Let us review each of these categories of emotional symptoms more carefully.

Mood Responses

These are the responses associated with dramatic changes in mood. Individuals experiencing mood responses tend to become sullen or testy or irritable. Their mood is significantly altered by stress and anxiety. Someone who is normally talkative may not speak. Someone who is normally friendly may not mingle in social situations. Mood affects feelings, language and attitude. The most significant thing is that mood swings are very noticeable.

We sometimes say, "He is not himself." Or, "She is in a bad mood." Sometimes we are not even aware of these changes in ourselves. Or, if we are aware, we may not be motivated to change them. It is as if our bodies assume these mood changes as some sort of temporary personality change. It often leads others to question, "What's bothering him/her?"

Emotionally Labile Responses

These are responses which cause individuals to cry easily or yell easily. We can become very fragile or temperamental when under stress, resulting in our emotions overwhelming us. How often have you heard an anxious person say, "I can't stop crying." Or, "I can't stop yelling at everybody."

These extreme emotional feelings are a clear sign of stress. Our emotional feelings override other body functions. We tend to demonstrate the emotion which best aligns with our intense feelings. We cry if we are sad. We shake if we are afraid. We become angry if we perceive to be threatened. This mobilization contributes to the "fight or flight" response.

Feelings of Losing Control

Many of the emotions associated with test anxiety often relate to fear of losing of control. Such fear leads to feelings of panic and an almost out-of-body experience. We feel totally overwhelmed and powerless. Have you ever heard someone say, "I am becoming unglued"? Or, "I am falling apart?" This fear of loss of control is one of the most significant contributors to poor test performance. We open the test booklet and discover that we do not know the answers to the first several questions. We look ahead at the next 150 items, and our anxiety turns to panic.

 ## Mental/Cognitive Component

The third and final component of the Test Anxiety Triangle is the mental or cognitive component. The symptoms most often associated with this component are:

- **Irrational thinking**
- **Feelings of failure or rejection**
- **Forgetfulness and memory loss**
- **Loss of concentration and focus**

Once again, let's examine each of these symptoms more carefully.

Irrational Thinking

Statements that we say to ourselves that increase feelings of anxiety comprise irrational thinking. These statements use faulty logic or irrational logic, and are often based on mistaken beliefs. Unfortunately, when we are anxious, we cling to these beliefs and they control our emotions and our actions.

Irrational thinking translates into erroneous cause and

effect statements. For example, "Since I failed the last English test, I will certainly fail the next one." Or, "Since I don't like Biology, I know I will fail the midterm."

Feelings of Failure or Rejection

Some would argue that feelings of failure and rejection are basically one in the same. Namely, if you are afraid to fail, it is because you are afraid of what others will think of you. In this way, failure is associated with socially based anxieties.

However, some people are afraid of failure regardless of what anyone else thinks. Perhaps because of perfectionistic thinking or a strong ego, some adults and children are driven by success and the mere thought of failure is traumatic. Instead of being willing to learn from their mistakes and errors, they want to "fall on the sword."

Forgetfulness and Memory Loss

Perhaps the most troublesone problem associated with the cognitive component of test anxiety is forgetfulness and memory loss. Most high stakes tests require a high degree of memorization of facts. When test anxiety becomes strong, we lose our ability to remember. Our mind literally goes blank. That is why I feel so strongly about reducing high levels of test anxiety. It's not just about feeling less stressful, it's about performing better.

Loss of Concentration and Focus

When we are stressed, our ability to concentrate and focus on what is before us is greatly reduced. Have you ever driven a car when you were very upset? I remember once driving my wife to the emergency room in the middle of the night. When I arrived at the hospital, I had no recollection whatsoever of how I got there. My wife later told me that I drove through two red lights! How can students concentrate on a very demanding timed test if they are highly anxious? The answer is, not very well.

Post-Testing Phase

As soon as a student closes the examination booklet, the post-testing phase begins, but the lingering effects of test anxiety do not end. As with the earlier two phases, the impact of test anxiety on the test-taker is greatly influenced by the individual's characteristics and the environments he/she negotiates, as explained in Chapter 2. If students leave the exam site with perceived feelings of failure and those perceptions are somehow reinforced by others, they can end up with a continuing anxiety problem, even though the test is over. Furthermore, this type of post-test anxiety can become a vicious cycle. If the actual test results confirm the individual's worst fear, it has the potential to become a negative self-fulfilling prophecy for the next examination. (Refer to Chart XV on a subsequent page in this chapter).

Of course when a test-taker performs poorly, anxiety may not be the primary contributor. Other factors might have been more influential. Perhaps the teacher did not initially present the content well, or the teacher did not review the material effectively, or the student may have reviewed the wrong content for the test. However, students who feel that they "blew the exam" might not be so analytical about *why* and *how* they failed. Instead, they are often left with generalized feelings of failure and disappointment. When the actual test results come in and confirm these feelings, it becomes imprinted as an emotionally traumatic event. This imprint sets the stage for an even higher level of test anxiety for the next high stakes testing situation.

High Stakes/High Expectations

The extent to which students' performances on high stakes tests affects society's view of them is truly amazing. Self-fulfilling prophecies can work both in negative and in positive directions.

A technology specialist working in the offices of the Educational Testing Service accidentally altered the programming software just as the College Entrance Examination Boards data on one Henry Carson was being scored.

Henry was an average high school student who was unsure of himself and his abilities. Had it not been for this programming error, Henry's scores would have been average or less. But the error changed all of that. For the scores which emerged from the computer were amazing 800's in both the verbal and quantitative areas.

When the scores reached Henry's school, the word of his giftedness spread like wildfire. Teachers began to reevaluate their gross underestimation of him. Counselors trembled at the thought of neglecting such a talent. And, college admissions officers began to recruit Henry for their schools.

New worlds opened for Henry. And as they opened, he started to grow as a person and as a student. Once he became aware of his potential and began to be treated differently by the significant people in his life, a form of self-fulfilling prophecy took place. Henry gained in confidence and began "to put his mind in the way of great things"... Henry became one of the best men of his generation.

> - Adapted from a story by William W. Purkey, and included with permission of author.

It is unfortunate that the results of high stakes testing play such a major role in the way we perceive others and ourselves. Alfie Kohn talks about the various factors that children attribute to their successes or failures in school, such as effort, ability, luck, and the level of difficulty of the task.

Teachers and parents most often focus on *effort* as the primary cause of success or failure in school and on tests. It is certainly the most controllable of the four types of attributes. Our entire society has been built on the belief that if you work hard enough anything is possible. Therefore, we impress upon children the importance of applying themselves, preparing, reviewing, studying, and working as hard as they can. We want children as test- takers to be positive and optimistic with the highest expectations for success. Simply put, think positive and be positive! Easier said than done.

Chart XIV

Types of Attribution

Type	Success	Failure
Effort	"I tried hard"	"I didn't study"
Ability	"I'm smart"	"I'm stupid"
Luck	"I was lucky"	"I am jinxed"
Level of Difficulty	"The test was very hard"	"The test was easy"

Post Traumatic Test Disorder

Imagine a child arrives home on a given day—or over several days, since some high stakes tests are given on multiple days—and faces the testing inquisition:

- "Well, how was the test?"
- "Was it harder than you thought?"
- "Was it like the practice tests?"
- "Do you think you studied enough?"
- "How did you do?"
- "Did you pass?"
- "When will you get the results?"

Pity the poor kid who comes home feeling that he/she blew the test, and faces these questions in rapid fire. Imagine how parents and peers can contribute to this child's stress level! I've coined a new term for this – Post Traumatic *Test* Disorder—a disorder that arises out of the emotional trauma associated with the aftermath of a test that a student feels that he/she has failed.

The concept of Post Traumatic Stress Disorder is most often associated with a particular set of symptoms that appear after a tragic and/or life-threatening event—like Jeremy and the lion. Symptoms usually include:

- recurring and distressing thoughts about the event
- nightmares and/or flashbacks reliving the traumatic event
- the development of a phobia toward the situation, event or object
- increased anxiety in general
- difficulty concentrating or paying attention

In the case of Post Traumatic *Test* Disorder, the symptoms are modified to include:

- persistent feelings of failure and poor self-worth
- an avoidance of test-taking and/or courses associated with the test's content
- difficulty concentrating or paying attention
- increased anxiety towards school and schoolwork
- increased anxiety in social situations

The best way to explain Post Traumatic Test Disorder is to recognize that it is a vicious cycle that, if not broken, will lead to chronic stress and test phobia. In other words, test anxiety *contributes* to "perceived" (or actual) poor performance on the exam which in turn *leads* to heightened feelings of failure, which are then *confirmed* by the test results. This series of events leads to increased stress and, ultimately, to test avoidance and possibly phobia. This vicious cycle, as illustrated in Chart XV, can only be broken by taking control of the situation and developing a plan. Understanding this problem and executing an effective plan to address it can best be accomplished through an explanation of how our basic needs affect motivation and behavior.

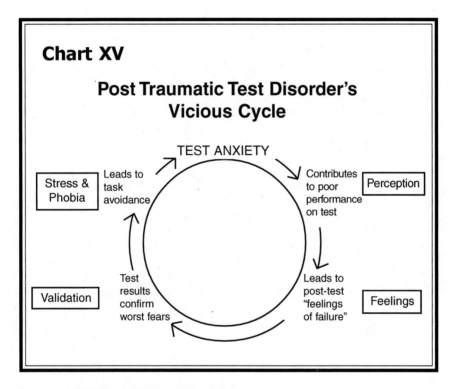

Chart XV

Post Traumatic Test Disorder's Vicious Cycle

TEST ANXIETY

Stress & Phobia — Leads to task avoidance

Contributes to poor performance on test — Perception

Test results confirm worst fears

Validation

Leads to post-test "feelings of failure" — Feelings

Choice Theory

Dr. William Glasser, author of *Reality Therapy, Schools Without Failure,* and *The Quality School,* developed a psychological theory that helps us explain human behavior called Choice Theory. This theory argues that all behavior is driven by the fulfillment of one or more of the following five basic needs: survival, a sense of belonging, power, freedom and fun. Glasser argues that these needs are built into our genetic structure and all of our motivation is derived from the need to satisfy them. Unlike Abraham Maslow's well known framework of needs, Choice Theory's basic needs are not hierarchial. Other than survival, which is a physical need, the other four needs are psychological and, as such, vary in strength and intensity based on many factors. Our feelings provide feedback on whether our behaviors are getting us what we want and/or need. Thus, we choose behaviors based on feelings. We either feel good or feel bad based on the extent to which we are satisfying one or more of these basic needs.

Chart XVI

Choice Theory's Basic Needs

Survival	physical needs
Sense of Belonging	acceptance, love, friendship
Power	knowledge, expertise, recognition
Freedom	choices, options, independence
Fun	laughter, happiness, joy

Life's experiences cause us to store many need-satisfying memories in what William Glasser calls our *quality world*. It is like a scrapbook of pictures or perceptions in our heads that is personalized for each individual. These perceptions drive our behavior because we believe that striving to obtain or maintain these perceptions is essential to a need-fulfilling life. A loving mother, close friends or a cherished pet could be the pictures in the quality world of a young child who has a strong sense of belonging. A driver's license, a part-time job after school, and choosing a college to attend could be the pictures in the quality world of an adolescent who has a need for freedom. The ability to master a new computer program or solve a difficult problem could be pictures that relate to fulfilling the need for power. Going to a party, playing with friends or going on vacation may be images that fulfill the need for fun.

The value of Choice Theory is that it helps us better understand how a student with even a mild case of post traumatic test disorder behaves. Tests and the test-taking experience are not pictures in that student's quality world. The perception of failing a test is not at all need-fulfilling. Instead of a sense of a belonging, there is a sense of failure and rejection. Instead of a sense of power, there is a sense of incompetence. Instead of feeling freer, the perceived or real failure on the test limits choices and options—like low scores on the SAT in relation to getting into a specific college. And certainly, failing a test is no fun. It is a painful experience that can lead to feelings of despair.

To counteract these feelings and address basic needs, students must choose to perform need-satisfying behaviors. The simplest choice for students with post traumatic test disorder is avoidance. They never want to take a test again, or worse, never want to go back to school. As adults, we need to help children and adolescents recognize their feelings and help them set goals and develop plans to put pictures of tests and success in school back into their quality worlds. But they must ultimately choose this. Glasser makes it very clear that coercion of any kind (carrot or stick) will not work. Students have to be helped to recognize that they, and they alone, can put pictures in or take pictures out of their quality worlds. Through goal setting, counseling, and other supportive techniques, test-takers can take control of their fears and anxieties and motivate themselves. Several strategies addressing post-testing anxiety are presented in Chapter 7.

Chart XVII

Basic Needs and Test Anxiety

Basic Needs	Source of Emotional Problem	Negative Self-Talk (Examples)
Sense of Belonging	Excessive need for approval (fear of rejection)	"I must please others." "I must not disappoint my parents and teachers."
Power	Excessive need for perfection and/or accomplishment (fear of failure)	"I cannot make mistakes." "I must get a high score." "If I fail, I am a failure."
Freedom	Excessive need for control (fear of loss of control)	"I must be in control." "What happens if I fail?"
Fun	Excessive need for enjoyment (fear of unhappiness and depression)	"It's only a test." "What's the big deal?"

Summary

In conclusion, I hope that this chapter has furthered your understanding of test anxiety. To review, our framework uses three phases—pre-testing, test-in-progress, and post-testing. Each phase carries particular challenges as it relates to reducing anxiety.

You learned that differentiated instruction and the use of the theory of Multiple Intelligences are critically important in the pre-testing phase. By recognizing and addressing the differences in children, we as educators and parents can better teach and prepare students for tests. The more confident they are with their understanding and mastery of content, the less likely they will develop test anxiety.

You also learned that Emotional Intelligence plays an important role in our understanding of test anxiety. The need to be aware of and regulate our emotions is a critical factor in a successful test anxiety reduction plan, especially since emotions peak as one approaches and experiences the test-in-progress phase.

The Test Anxiety Triangle model moved us from the theoretical to the practical reality of the test-taking experience. The model explains how physical, emotional, and mental/cognitive symptoms contribute to poor performance on tests.

Finally, the post-testing phase also carries with it a set of unique challenges. Anxiety does not end when the test booklet is closed. Post traumatic test disorder (or degrees of it) can set into motion many negative consequences for the future. Choice Theory helps better explain how failing a test (or perceptions of failure) can lead to avoidance behaviors.

Now comes the most important part. Chapters 5, 6, and 7 present specific strategies and techniques that can be implemented by teachers, parents, and kids in school and at home. We have set the stage, now let the play begin!

Chapter 5
Pre-Testing Strategies

To begin, we will examine strategies that should be taught and implemented in the time before a high stakes test is administered. The following strategies help students prepare effectively for the test and provide a means of reducing the associated test anxiety:

- **Sending positive messages**
- **Utilizing effective study skills**
- **Developing good study habits**
- **Taking practice tests**
- **Providing tutoring**

Sending Positive Messages

The verbal messages that we, as adults, send to kids are critical to creating an environment in which test anxiety is either nourished or reduced. Teachers and parents each play a major role in influencing this pre-testing environment. Let's explore what each of these two stakeholder groups can do to reduce the often high degree of hysteria that sometimes surrounds high stakes testing.

What Teachers Can Do

Teachers need to ask themselves an important series of questions about what *verbal messages* they are conveying (consciously or unconsciously) to their students. They should begin by asking themselves the following questions:

- What words do I use to convey the importance of the upcoming test?
- What do I say about the purpose(s) of the test?
- What do I say about how the results of the test will be used?
- Do I talk about (and focus on) passing or failing?
- When do I begin talking about the important upcoming test? (How far in advance should I announce it?)

In other words, what teachers say, as well as what they do, directly contributes to the level of test anxiety felt by the students. Teachers need to be very reflective about their comments. I recommend that they script out the points that they want to convey. The more thoughtful and purposeful they are with their messages, the greater the likelihood that they will address and ultimately reduce pre-test anxiety.

Read the following Example #1, which is a statement made by Mrs. Jones to her fourth grade class about an upcoming test. As you read the announcement, make note of the types of messages that she conveys to the students. Pay particular attention to the words Mrs. Jones chooses, as well as the time frame for the announcement. Furthermore, imagine that you are a test-anxious student and reflect on the emotions that such an announcement may bring to the surface.

Example # 1

Mrs. Jones' 4th Grade Class Announcement

Good morning, boys and girls. I want to make an announcement about an English/Language Arts test that you will be taking in a few months. In January (it's now October), a very important test will be given to all students in 4th grade throughout our state. The test will be timed and given over several days.

We all want you to do well on this test, so I will be working over the next three months to prepare you. We will cover examples of the types of questions that will be on the test and we will be taking some practice tests to help you become more familiar with it. Our principal, Mr. Franklin, will be holding an assembly for 4th graders later this month to share with you how important it is for all of you to do your best on this test. Also, your parents will be receiving more information before Thanksgiving so that they will better understand these tests. Boys and girls, do you have any questions?

Now I would like you to read Example # 2 on the next page. This announcement is being made by Mrs. Simmons, who teaches two doors down from Mrs. Jones. Mrs. Simmons is preparing her students for the same English/Language Arts test, but she approaches it differently. Once again, please pay attention to the words used, and try to reflect on the emotions that could be emerging from Mrs. Simmons' students as she announces the upcoming test.

Example # 2

Mrs. Simmons' 4th Grade Class Announcement

Good morning, boys and girls. You know that we learn in many different ways and, because of that, schools need to measure how well students have learned in many different ways. You know that sometimes I give you projects to do, and you are all working on your math and science portfolios. But another way to measure what we have learned is by taking paper and pencil tests.

Our state education department wants to better understand how well 4th graders across the state are doing in English/Language Arts. So in January (it's now late November), all 4th graders in our school and schools across the state will be taking a test. Although we want all of you to do well, it is only one type of test. It does, however, have several different parts and you will have a chance to select correct answers to questions as well as read stories and write about them.

It will be fun to see how our class will do. We will practice some examples of items on this test before Christmas. Once again, if you hear anything about this test from 5th grade schoolmates who may have taken this test last year, or from your parents, or you just want to talk about it, please see me.

You are all good learners. And this test is just one of many ways for you to show us how much you have learned.

At first glance, the announcement in Example #1 seems pretty benign and factual. Mrs. Jones gives information four months before the test with an emphasis on the importance of the test. An announcement about the assembly with the principal, Mr. Franklin, and a parent meeting certainly indicate that this test is pretty important. But Mrs. Jones' announcement is lacking in terms of positive messages.

In Example #2, Mrs. Simmons also emphasizes the importance of the test, but acknowledges that it is only one of many ways to measure students' learning. She makes her announcement well over a month later and makes no mention of the principal's assembly or upcoming parent meeting. Mrs. Simmons also does one other important thing. She asks her students to speak to her if others talk to them about the test. This request provides the opportunity for her students to seek her out, either if a 5th grader tries to scare one of her students about the difficulty of the upcoming test, or if a student's parent starts talking about it at home, possibly raising the level of anxiety.

Teachers need to work with their building administration to develop a clear, positive support system of communication with kids and their parents. That communication must contribute to reducing the high levels of anxiety often associated with high stakes tests. How announcements are made, when they are made, and the words used are very important, especially for the students who are more prone to anxiety. All teachers really want to be positive and supportive. But, they may not recognize how even the apparently positive message can be inadequate at best and counterproductive at worst.

Chart XVIII

The Messages Teachers Convey

Positive Messages	Less Positive Messages
• There are multiple ways to learn/multiple ways to assess.	• This test will show us what you know.
• Practice helps us to prepare.	• Practice makes perfect.
• Do your best. We believe in you.	• Try your best. That's all anyone can do.
• Let me know if others talk to you about the test.	• If you have any questions, let me know.
• It is normal to worry about tests.	• Don't worry, everything will work out.
• If you do not do as well as you expected, we will find out why and work on ways to help you in the future.	• If you fail, we will tell you what items you missed.

Remember, teachers cannot control all of the information that students will process about the upcoming tests, but I argue that they are the most influential in *setting the tone*. If teachers look and act scared or panicky about a test, they will transmit that fear to their students. The best anxiety reducing messages delivered to students about upcoming tests should include the following positive messages:

- We learn in different ways and we measure learning in different ways.
- A paper and pencil test is only one way to measure what we know.
- We will practice and prepare.
- We expect that you will do well.
- It is OK if you feel worried.
- Speak to me, as your teacher, if you have any questions, concerns, or worries about the test.

Notice how these points relate to the material that we covered in Chapter 4 (i.e., differentiated instruction, Multiple Intelligences, Emotional Intelligence, and Choice Theory).

What Parents Can Do

Like teachers, parents can be very important in the pre-testing environment. Regardless of the age of their child, parents should never underestimate the messages that they send. Read each of the following comments made by a parent to his or her child:

Statement A — "You better study for the math test next week. I heard that it is very hard."

Statement B — "Your brother did poorly on the SATs and it prevented him from getting into the college he wanted."

Statement C — "You know that English is not your favorite subject, so hit the books."

Statement D — "You better worry about next week's test, you failed the last one."

What is your impression? Are these statements helpful? Let's look more closely. The messages embedded in the statements listed above focus on motivation. Each statement could be restated as follows:

Statement A	"The test is hard, you better prepare."
Statement B	"If you do poorly, it will hurt you."
Statement C	"You must study hard for things you don't like or are not good at."
Statement D	"Your past experience should teach you to prepare better and work harder"

No matter how accurate these statements may be, they do not effectively help students prepare or study, because they are apt to increase anxiety more than they increase the child's motivation to study. Consider the following restatements as questions:

Statement A	"Do you know what is covered on the math test? Do you feel prepared?"
Statement B	"The SAT is important to college admission, however, did you know that it's only one factor?"
Statement C	"How will you prepare for the English test given that it's not your favorite subject?"
Statement D	"How do you feel about next week's test?"

Asking questions is sometimes a better way for parents to send messages because well structured questions are less critical in the tone and are more apt to foster a discussion or dialogue. Asking rather than telling, listening rather than talking, engaging in a dialogue rather than lecturing will produce a greater likelihood of success—both in terms of motivation to study, and in terms of anxiety reduction.

Effective Study Skills

One of the best ways to prepare for any final assessment, whether it be an oral presentation in front of the class or a major end-of-year exam, is to effectively study. Note that I said, *effectively* study. I hear many parents who tell me that their kids spend hours studying, yet seem to perform poorly on tests. I believe that this poor performance in many cases is a result of the ineffective use of study skills and poor study habits.

Unfortunately, teachers do not spend enough time teaching their students how to study and prepare. As a result, students know what they need to review (the content) for the upcoming test, but they really don't know how (the process) to study the material. Professionals who work with children who have special learning needs know the importance of teaching study skills and strategies. In fact, they incorporate these strategies into the curriculum that they teach.

Study skills are not innate. They need to be taught and practiced. The more prepared students feel for a test, the less likely that anxiety will interfere once the test is underway. In this way, study skills are truly an anxiety-reducing approach.

I believe that the following effective study skills are helpful for all students, but particularly those who have heightened levels of test anxiety. Of course, the age/grade level of the student should be taken into account when determining the appropriateness of these study skills. I will try to explain each strategy briefly.

Classroom Notetaking

To prepare for any test, it is first assumed that the students have been exposed to the content. Even though prior learning plays a role, most teachers present content in class that is later assessed in some fashion, usually through written tests. The majority of the teaching in our schools is still "chalk and talk," where teachers present orally to students while jotting down on the blackboard some key concepts while kids sit at their desks with notepads and textbooks open.

Although cooperative learning and other approaches have gained popularity in our elementary schools, in most middle and high schools you will still find the teacher up in front of the class "talking", "asking questions", and "writing" on the board—the old "sage on the stage" approach.

As I mentioned in the Introduction, my goal is to help reduce high levels of test anxiety so that kids can perform better on mandated standardized, and other high stakes tests. It is not my goal to preach about how schools should teach—well, not totally. I did slip in the preceding chapter information on differentiated instruction, didn't I?

The point is that notetaking in class is a very important skill, and how these notes are organized plays a key role when later studying for a test. Here are some tips that can be taught to students:

- **Use abbreviations** to save time and simplify notetaking. History becomes "hist." Inches become "in." Ounces become "oz." Names, terms, or phrases could be shortened by taking the first letter or two of each word. If abbreviations become too confusing, then after the notes are taken, a simple legend may need to be written in a corner of your notebook. If abbreviations are not possible, then use parts of words, short phrases or symbols (e.g., = means equal, w/o means without, etc.)

- **Listen for key words** that the teacher uses that can identify an important point. Anything that he or she breaks down by consecutive or progressive points is critical to note. Students will recognize these points when teachers use words such as "first", "second", "third", or other transition terms (e.g. "next").

These types of words that indicate individual points should signal to the student that he or she should number or denote them in their notes. Pretend the following paragraph represents a teacher's lecture in school:

The message from one peer to another does not, in and of itself, inherently carry a positive or negative message. Three factors contribute to a message being taken by an individual as positive or negative in terms of reducing high levels of anxiety. First, the message itself—does it convey a feeling that is positive, supportive, and anxiety-reducing? Second, the relationship with the peer—the extent to which one values the peer's perspective or opinion on a given topic. And third, the interpretation of the message by the individual receiving it. Although the peer's intention may be to reduce anxiety and to be positive in tone, the interpretation of the individual receiving it may actually cause it to have the opposite effect.

If you were to take notes, they might be written as follows:

> Peer messages
> 1. the mess itself—is it + or -
> 2. relation to peer—value peer or opinion (+ or -)
> 3. interpret of the mess—how is it received

Note how the numbering of each point facilitated notetaking. Also, note the use of abbreviated terms and symbols.

- **Listen to the teacher's voice.** The inflection, volume and tone can be important variables to guide notetaking. Try to distinguish important points in a lecture or presentation by asking the following questions: Does the teacher raise his/her voice level when an important point is made? Does he/she repeat important points? Does he/she give an example immediately after an important point is made? Of course, teachers lecture and present differently. Some have monotone voices that make it more difficult to decipher changes in inflection or emphasis. Also, listen for teacher pronouncements. If the teacher says, "This is important," or "This is critical," or "Remember this," or "This will be on the test," put your pen or pencil to your notepad.

- **Watch the teacher.** If he/she writes key points on the blackboard, those are no-brainers—write them in your notes. Also, if the teacher points to his/her fingers to identify key points by saying, "The number one reason...The number two reason...The number three reason...", write those points down.

- **Review your notes.** I often hear students say that they cannot read their notes (legibility) or understand what the abbreviations or symbols they have used mean. It is critical to review one's notes within a reasonable time frame after they are taken. It will also allow the notetaker time to ask the teacher questions and/or to check the textbook for clarification.

How Teachers Can Help With Notetaking

If teachers provide one or more of the following strategies, their students will be better note-takers.

- **Always state the purpose of the lesson**, and write it on the blackboard. It is best written as an outcome. For example, instead of writing or saying:
  "Today we are going to talk about the digestive system,"
  it is better to say:
  "Today you will learn to name the parts of the digestive system."
  Specificity does make a big difference.

- **Break the content being delivered into smaller units** and number them if at all possible. For example, instead of talking about the different branches of government, state that there are three branches of government:
  1. judicial
  2. legislative
  3. executive
  Organization and order can greatly help students.

- **Prompt or clearly identify points** your students should write in their notes by making statements like:

"This is very important to remember."
"Write this down..."
"This will be on the test."
"You will need to know this."
This strategy relates to the term *teacher pronouncements,* mentioned earlier.

- **Repeat important points and/or give illustrations or examples.** The more time you spend on an important point, the more likely that the student will identify it as important to note. Also, examples are not only helpful to learning, but they give students another reference point for notetaking.

- **Use visuals wherever possible.** We know that many students learn better visually than auditorily. Therefore, the use of an overhead, blackboard, or written handout can be invaluable to students, especially those who are anxious about the content you are presenting.

- **Teach and practice notetaking** by reviewing with your students what they should have recorded in their notes after a lecture or presentation. By concretely showing students what they should or should not have recorded, they will be better able to differentiate the two later. Explicit teaching is perhaps the best single approach to effective notetaking. Each teacher varies in his/her teaching style, so help your students to better understand what you are specifically looking for when they take notes in your class.

- **Review students' notes periodically.** It is important that your students take effective notes and do not just sit there and doodle. Therefore, a teacher has a responsibility to review students' notes and provide constructive feedback on a periodic basis, also encouraging them to write legibly.

Notetaking from Textbooks

Taking notes from textbooks is similar to taking notes in class because in both instances the student has to differentiate what is important to note from what is not. The difference is that most textbooks provide more obvious cues to help students to differentiate what should be noted.

Some textbooks *italicize* important points, or print them in a bolder font, as I have done in this book. Also, textbooks organize content using headings and subheadings. Graphics may be utilized in an effort to organize the content being provided. Furthermore, there isn't the same time pressure as there is with a teacher lecturing. You can take the book home and work on your notes at your own pace. Since textbooks in most elementary, middle and high schools are reused year-to-year, students may not be able to highlight or write notes in them. Therefore, like taking notes in class, students need some guidelines on how to take notes from textbooks. Sometimes parents purchase a second copy of the textbook so their child can "mark it up." Of course, college is another story. The cost of textbooks is so high that students try not to mark them up so that they can be re-sold after the semester ends.

The following notetaking techniques can help students not only with notes from textbooks but also when completing book reports or reviewing other reference materials:

- **Use titles of chapters and subheadings to construct an outline.** For example, look back at Chapter 1 of this book, which "set the stage" by covering a number of related but different topics about testing. By just using the headings, you could provide a framework for an outline as follows:

Beginning Outline (Chapter 1)

Daddy, Daddy, I Can't Sleep...
- Valuing High Stakes Tests
- The Explosion of Testing
- Teaching to the Test
- No Child Left Behind—Test Them All

Next, briefly describe each section of a textbook by a short phrase. Again, using Chapter 1 as an example:

More Detailed Outline (Chapter 1)

Daddy, Daddy, I Can't Sleep...

- Author tells story about his daughter not sleeping due to worry.
    - Valuing High Stakes Tests
        - society values doing well on tests
    - The Explosion of Testing
        - growing because of increasing accountability
    - Teaching to the Test
        - not bad in itself
        - depends on the test and what it measures
    - No Child Left Behind——Test Them All
        - testing modifications can be used
        - new law has great impact

When textbooks are loaded with facts that need to be memorized, as opposed to the more conversational style of this book, students need a more detailed outline that follows this type of structure:

<u>Chapter Heading</u>

- Subchapter (section) Heading
  Listing of related facts

- Next Subchapter (section) Heading
  Listing of related facts

- **Read the opening and closing section of each chapter carefully.** If they outline the important points of the chapter, then these opening and closing sections should align with students' notes.

- **Answer questions at the end of a chapter.** Many textbooks have questions at the end of every chapter, like a short quiz. If the textbook does not have questions, then students should try and create some of their own.

Recording Notes

Many parents ask, "How should students record notes?" It is best to take notes in a composition book, three-ring binder, on index cards, or on a laptop computer?" There is no easy answer to that question. In fact, there is no single answer. Some would argue that *how* notes are kept is as important as the notes themselves. This issue of organization is covered later in this chapter under Developing Good Study Habits. Here are some helpful hints:

Chart XIX

Notetaking Recording Systems

Type	**Advantages**	**Disadvantages**	**Best Use**
Composition Book	Pages cannot be easily lost	Hard to add new material	Writing logs
3-Ring Binder	Easy to set up dividers and to add and subtract pages	Pages can be lost and harder to carry	Notetaking for multiple subjects
Index Cards	Memorization of discrete facts (like flash cards); small and easy to carry	Easy to lose; cards can get out of order	Oral reports
Laptop Computer/ Alpha Smart-Type Device	Easy entry (if good at key-boarding); can reformulate notes easily	Not easy or practical to carry; cost	Longer reports and projects

The ability to retrieve and access notes is very important, especially for students with attentional, activity-level or organizational difficulties. Whatever recording system works best should be established and periodically reviewed to ensure that it is the most effective. What worked in elementary school may not be as helpful with the departmentalized approach of a middle school. Similarly, what worked in high school might need to be adjusted in large college lecture halls.

Chart XX

Helpful Notetaking Strategies
(Summary)

Student Strategies

- Use abbreviations/short phrases
- Listen for key words (e.g., first, second, next, etc.)
- Listen to the teacher's voice (i.e., inflection, volume and tone) and for pronouncements
- Watch for written points on the blackboard, overheads or handouts

Teacher Strategies

- State (and write) purpose of lesson
- Break content into smaller units
- Prompt and identify what is important
- Repeat and give examples of important points
- Use visuals wherever possible
- Teach and practice notetaking with your class
- Review students' notes periodically

Textbook Strategies

- Use titles and sub-chapter headings as an outline
- Describe content under each heading in short phrases
- Sort facts to be memorized by section
- Review introduction and summary of each chapter
- Answer questions at the end of chapter or develop your own questions

Graphic Organizers

I am a better visual learner than auditory learner. If you were to invite me to your house for a party, I would much prefer a map being drawn than a list of oral directions telling me to take the third traffic light after the four-way stop sign, one mile after getting off the exit ramp, etc.

One of the best ways for visual learners to organize information and notes is by using graphic organizers. Graphic organizers come in many shapes, sizes and designs. Two popular types include:
- web chart
- flow chart

A web chart is a way to array information visually using a series of interconnecting designs (usually circles or ovals). The size and position of the circles and ovals, as well as their relationship to one another in terms of the interconnecting lines all have significance. This type of visual array can help students see the connections between concepts, making it easier to remember and retrieve learned information.

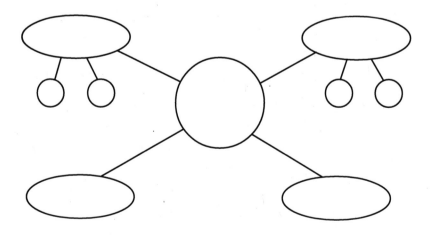

A sample of how a web chart on test anxiety might be drawn is presented as follows:

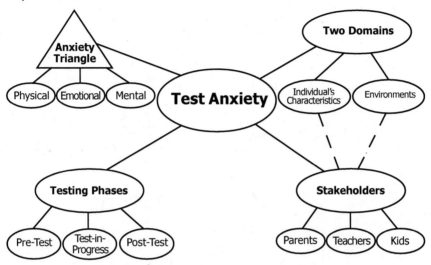

A flow chart is a more sequential pattern of boxes like a table of organization for a company. It is most helpful to show how things are organized or how things are processed.

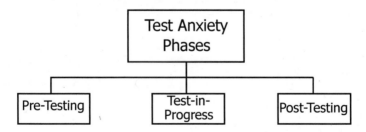

Flow charts are more helpful when organizing information in a sequential and/or hierarchial fashion. Once again, the material is interrelated in different ways so that some boxes would connect with others and some would not. In addition to using web charts and flow charts to relate important information, there are a number of other graphic organizers or aids that students need to understand and interpret as part of their preparation for tests. It is also important that students be able to interpret and use tables, diagrams, maps, pictographs, etc.

Pie Charts

Bar Graphs

Line Graph

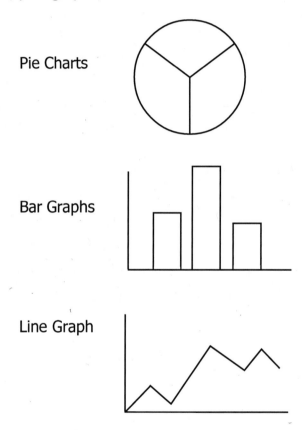

Improving Memory

As was stated earlier, the ability to recall information, concentrate and focus is severely reduced when anxiety is high. Therefore, any way to improve the ability to retrieve facts and information during the high anxiety of testing will greatly help. As I cover three basic strategies, think back to our discussion of Multiple Intelligences and how kids are smart (and how they learn) in different ways.

- **Rhymes and songs** - These are powerful ways to remember for those who are good auditory learners, or who like rhythm and music. Creating rhymes and songs to retrieve information can be very beneficial and fun. To this day I remember which months have 30 days versus 31 because of the childhood rhyme. Perhaps you remember Columbus sailing the ocean blue in 1492, or "i" before "e" except after "c", or "Doe a deer, a female deer, Ray a drop of golden sun..."

    When my children were in elementary school, they learned all of the Presidents of the United States (in order!) through a song that their music teacher taught them. If I ask my daughter who the tenth president was, she would sing the song and count on her fingers to give me the answer. The power of rhymes and songs cannot be underestimated. Think of how shows like *Sesame Street* use the power of rhymes and songs to help millions of kids learn and remember helpful and important information. Patricia Wolfe, author of *Brain Matters*, emphasizes the important role that music, rhyme and rhythm play in enhancing memory and the recall of information.

- **Visualization** - In the next chapter I will cover how visualization can be used to reduce anxiety. However, visualization can also be used to help remember content and information. In combination with web or flow charts, or other graphic organizers and aids, one can more easily retrieve information from visual images. The adage that "a picture is worth a thousand words" is still true. Visual images, pictures, drawings and the like can greatly help students retrieve information.

• **Acronyms** - Perhaps nowhere in the world are acronyms used more than in the bureaucracy of a school.

The PTA is having a meeting on IEPs and invited UFT representatives to discuss how the new SBC affects children with ADD.

The legend is as follows:

PTA = Parent Teacher Association
IEP = Individual Education Program
UFT = United Federation of Teachers
SBC = Standards-Based Curriculum
ADD = Attention Deficit Disorder

It's like alphabet soup. And each state has its own unique *soup d'jour*!

Nevertheless, acronyms or acrostic sentences to help students remember lengthy or complicated information can be quite helpful. Sometimes they are associated with a sentence. Try to remember the nine planets in the solar system. Taking the first letter of each word or concept greatly reduces the amount of material one needs to process, and helps trigger memory.

My very eager mother just served us nine pizzas. (Mercury, Venus, Earth, Mars, Jupiter, Saturn, Uranus, Neptune, and Pluto)

Acronyms, acrostic sentences, as well as some rhymes and phrases, are part of a larger class called *mnemonic* devices that aid memory and recall. Students or teachers often invent their own. It's not only fun, but it really works! The brain learns best through patterning and associations.

Accessing Information and Resources

There are several ways to access information and resources that can help with efforts to study and better understand material covered:

- Using the library
- Using information resources at home (e.g., encyclopedias, dictionaries, atlases, maps, magazines and newspaper articles, etc.)
- Using the Internet
- Using CD-Roms and other computer-based resources
- Using tutors or peers in either a one-on-one setting or in study groups

Teaching students how to find and use resources can not only support previously learned material, but can also be used for the development of essays, reports and projects.

Developing Good Study Habits

Perhaps one of the most effective ways to reduce anxiety for those who are preparing for a test is to improve study habits. Although much has been written about study skills, the primary components of good study habits can be organized into the following areas:

- **Anticipatory planning** – Developing means to coordinate *how, when,* and *where* you are going to study, developing a schedule, and setting realistic goals.
- **Time management** – Self-monitoring your time and following your schedule.

• **Organizational skills** – Ensuring that you have organized all of your notes, handouts, and other materials needed to study appropriately.

Study habits can make the difference between a student having optimal levels of anxiety or having heightened levels of anxiety. The more we help a student understand the content and review the course material, the more confident the student will feel going into the exam.

Anticipatory Planning

Structuring how, when, and where a student is going to study is one of the most important prerequisites to developing effective study skills. If students do not anticipate and address these planning-related issues, their ability to use the study skills strategies will be greatly hampered. Developing good habits, like study skills, should be part of teachers' and parents' test preparation strategies. For example, Chart XXI identifies three aspects of anticipatory planning and a range of options that teachers, parents and students should consider.

How you study and with whom is largely dependent on personal preferences. Namely, do you prefer to study alone rather than in groups because you can focus better? Are you more likely to become distracted when studying with others? If you study with others, who are the best individuals to study with? Getting to better understand how you work best is critical to developing a positive environment for studying.

When you study is one of the most practical decisions that needs to be made. Once again, personal preferences, as well as other factors such as the availability of others to study with, play a critical role in choosing the best time.

Chart XXI

Anticipatory Planning
(Study Options)

How	With whom	Alone With a friend With a study group With your parents' help
When	The time	Early in the morning After school In the evening On weekends
Where	The location	At the kitchen table In the school library In the bedroom

When can you focus best—in the morning or in the evening? Before school or after school? Weekdays or weekends? Find the best times and stick to them. Many experts advocate the use of a calendar and most schools have planners which can help students block out set times for study. A daily, weekly or monthly planner can be a most effective tool for scheduling time to prepare for upcoming tests, homework, class projects and other assignments.

Where you study is equally important. If you cannot find an appropriate place to study, you will be unable to study well. Is it quiet? Is it comfortable? Do you have access to the needed resources to study? Does it minimize distractions? Whether it is a school library, a student lounge, a family room or a bedroom, the location must be conducive to studying. I cannot tell you how many children study with a television on in the room. Music in the background may not be as problematic unless the student is paying more attention to the lyrics than to their notetaking. Parents often identify obstacles that interfere with their children's lack of good study habits such as:

- constant telephone interruptions
- being bothered by younger siblings
- overextending in sports, clubs and other extracurricular activities, thus limiting study time
- competing priorities, such as a part-time job after school or on the weekend.

This is why anticipatory planning is essential. If issues such as *how, when,* and *where* to study are addressed in advance, it is less likely that these types of obstacles and interferences will occur.

Time Management

Monitoring the time allocated to studying is critical. How much time should I spend in total? How much time should I devote to different parts of the content that I need to study? How should I go about monitoring the best use of my study time? Am I "on schedule?" In addition to using planners and calendars to chart out a plan to study, the following may also be helpful:

- **Schedule in realistic time frames.** If you are effective at studying for an hour at a time, then do it. Two hours may be too long. You need to self-monitor your effectiveness. Certainly if you are tired, shorter blocks are better than longer blocks. Remember, it is not how long you study that matters, but how *well* you study. Study smarter, not harder.

- **Take frequent breaks.** Go for a short walk. Get a drink. Stretch. It is important to recognize that studying is hard work. It requires considerable attention and it consumes more energy than you ever imagined. If you work without breaks, your eyes are more likely to tire, you may get a headache and/or you will fatigue more quickly. Movement can enhance learning.

- **Vary what is studied.** Don't get bogged down on one highly repetitive task—like one that requires rote memorization. After a reasonable period of time, move from these highly repetitive and some-what boring study tasks to other types of tasks, such as preparing for essay or application questions. The brain functions best when there is variance in tasks.

- **Monitor your emotions and feelings.** If you are upset over some issue unrelated to the upcoming test, it is often advisable not study at that moment. If you are feeling anxious about the amount of studying you need to do to cover all of the necessary content, then try some of the anxiety-reducing techniques presented in the next chapter. Most of all, make maximum use of the time you do spend studying.

Organizational Skills

What good are well written notes if they cannot be found? How helpful can textbooks or handouts be if they are left in school? The ability to organize oneself is a par-ticularly critical part of good study habits. Students with attentional difficulties, hyperactivity or learning problems often have problems with the organization of their materials.

Organization relates to:

- the availability of the necessary materials and supplies
- the adherence to planned study times and locations
- a logical order or progression covering the required content.

Identify a method to keep all study materials in one place (e.g., a three-ring binder, a large accordion folder, etc.). Establish routines such as studying right after school, or just after dinner. Decide whether to study easy material first and progress to more difficult and complex content, or the reverse.

Taking Practice Tests

In the months and weeks leading up to a state mandated or other high stakes standardized test, teachers mobilize their resources. Principals remind teachers of the schedule of exams, practice tests are distributed, and staff development is offered to help teachers prepare.

Although parent-teacher organizations and district-wide newsletters often identify the schedule for the upcoming tests for parents (and students are also apprised) the greatest mobilization is by the teaching professionals. Like the allies preparing for D-Day and the Normandy Invasion, teachers develop a master plan. No. 2 pencils are sharpened, and the test prep environment begins!

Now, I'm not criticizing teachers who have an obligation to prepare their students. Once again, it is the *prudent* thing to do. The issue is the *degree* and *type* of pre-testing preparation. Teachers should ask the following questions that might help them identify whether the degree and type of their preparation is set at the appropriate level:

- How soon before a test is to be given do I begin my

formal preparation? (In other words, when do I stop teaching and begin reviewing material?)

- What percentage of classroom time is spent on teaching to the test?
- When do I start using practice tests?
- Are other academic or non-academic subjects not covered on the upcoming test sacrificed? (In other words, are schedules altered so as to eliminate other subjects from being taught during the test preparation period?)

The use of practice tests has become big business in the United States. Many companies produce booklets to provide a series of practice tests from the SATs to the Law Boards to all types of state-mandated high stakes tests. The selective use of these practice tests can be very helpful in assisting students to adequately anticipate what is going to be on the test. It also provides students the opportunity to familiarize themselves with the format of the test as well as the types of items and content to be covered.

Using practice tests to prepare students and reduce anxiety is parallel to the use of what psychologists call systematic desensitization (sometimes called *real-life* desensitization). In this process, individuals who have a phobia take small incremental steps that increase their exposure to the feared object or situation in order to reduce their anxiety. A hierarchy of steps are identified.

Each step in systematic desensitization increases exposure to the feared object or situation a bit more than the one before it. Risk-taking by the phobic individual systematically increases with each step. A therapist or support person helps the individual each step of the way until ultimately the phobic individual's anxiety is reduced sufficiently to a level where they can go it alone.

In the classic example, someone who is afraid of riding in elevators must first watch an elevator arriving and departing from a safe distance, then stand by a stationary elevator, then stand in a stationary elevator (first with a support person, then without a support person), then travel only one floor with a support person, and so forth.

For the highly test-anxious student, taking a practice test can be something like systematic desensitization. Although there are usually only a few truly test-phobic kids in a given class or grade, taking a test under simulated conditions can help many kids address their fears and anxieties. However, in most cases, teachers should focus on the following steps *before* they give a full blown practice test:

- **Select and review examples** of specific test items that students are likely to encounter (e.g. analogy questions for the SAT—Anxiety: Fear as _____: Reality)
- **Organize strategies** to help students "attack" various types of test questions (e.g. strategies to handle critical reading questions)
- **Illustrate the strategies** in class (model for students using examples)
- **Give simple assignments** in class and/or for homework that provide students multiple opportunities to practice (e.g. a handout of specific test items to practice at home)

The math teacher who helps kids read and interpret bar graphs, the social studies teacher who teaches kids to interpret political cartoons, the English teacher who gives homework on "comparing and contrasting" types of essays are all examples of assignments that provide practice for the test. The administration of a practice exam under real-life test conditions should be used sparingly and only after effort is placed on teaching the more targeted activities illustrated above. Too much time can be wasted giving practice tests in class to kids who really do not need this experience.

It's also important to note, as was stated earlier in Chapter 2, these sample or practice tests themselves can contribute to increased anxiety. The reason is that more time spent on these practice tests sends the message to students that the upcoming test is extremely important. Therefore, selecting the proper amount of advance preparation in relation to the test is crucial.

If a teacher feels that selected test-anxious students or students with special needs could benefit from the greater use of practice tests under exam conditions, then it might be advisable. Remember, however, to ensure that any student eligible for testing modifications has them available during the practice test as well.

Tutoring

The tutoring business is one of the fastest growing industries in education, and has greatly benefited from the rise of high stakes testing. Once a cottage industry for wealthier parents to access, tutoring is now coming to the masses—and in a big way! One of the new provisions of the No Child Left Behind (NCLB) Act mandates that states and local school districts identify tutoring and supplemental services to be made available (at school district expense) to students who fall below targeted levels. That's right—public schools can use federal monies to pay private tutoring companies! So, what had historically been a nice second source of after school income for high school math and science teachers is now becoming a major source of income for America's corporations.

Regardless of whether a tutor is supplied by a private company or is a high school honor student working with middle schoolers on Saturday mornings, a tutor needs to play multiple roles, including that of instructor, guide, and coach.

Tutor as Instructor

Obviously, the primary role of a tutor is to provide instruction. By that I mean not necessarily introducing new material or content as the classroom teacher would, but helping to explain and deepen understanding. In that way, a tutor's role is to provide content in a way that assists the learner to better comprehend what has been taught in a fashion that increases memory and retrieval.

Tutor as Guide

An effective tutor can help guide a learner through the maze of content in a way that facilitates learning and reduces anxiety. Namely, the tutor makes learning easier and more understandable. The learner, who may have initially been overwhelmed by the content, now feels that he/she has "a fighting chance". The tutor actually helps the learner believe that the material is learnable—something that the learner may not have believed before he/she started receiving tutoring. Thus, the tutor helps the learner manage the content, and together they negotiate the material.

Tutor as Coach (and Mentor)

The coaching part of tutoring has to do with developing independence and goal-setting. A tutor must help the learner learn and study independently, not just when the tutor is physically working with the learner. This type of independence and self-motivation is like the coach of a sports team inspiring his team to work harder and to strive to do their best. This effort addresses the emotional side of learning more than the cognitive side, helping the student build confidence and positive feelings about learning. Coaching and mentoring are connected. Sometimes, through the tutoring experience, the relationship changes from a coach to a mentor. The mentor's role elevates the personal side of the tutoring relationship. More than an instructor, guide or coach, the tutor becomes an ongoing support who the learner can call on and access for assistance outside of the designated tutoring session. It brings the tutoring to the highest level of relationship.

Planning the Tutoring Experience

The following represents the various types of tutoring that could be provided:

- helping with homework and projects
- preparing for a test
- reviewing content for increased understanding

The distinction between these three categories may seem artificial at first, but there are some clear differences in emphasis. Helping with homework projects and upcoming tests is much more targeted. Tutoring to increase understanding is often used when a learner is totally overwhelmed with the subject matter or wants to deepen understanding to do even better in a course. Regardless of the motivation to seek help, tutoring can greatly reduce anxiety for the learner. In *The Reading Tutor's Handbook*,

Jeanne and Gerald Schumm postulate that tutoring must be a well planned experience. They recommend that tutors must:

- **Understand their students' strengths and challenges**—develop a "profile" on the student and use informal assessments.

- **Set expectations**—especially about coming prepared, being on time and using appropriate behavior.

- **Set goals**—both short term and long term goals should be written and mutually agreed upon by the tutor and student.

- **Document progress**—a record-keeping system must be developed where activities are logged and progress is charted.

- **Set routines**—establish a regular and consistent schedule and routine, but also plan to include some special activity or surprise as well.

- **Use rewards**—select effective methods of encouragement, not necessarily tangible rewards.

- **Evaluate oneself**—be reflective, seek feedback and self-assess yourself as a tutor.

Chapter 6:
Test-in-Progress Strategies

You know the feeling. Your palms are sweaty. There are butterflies in your stomach. You press so hard to fill in the bubble on the answer sheet that the No. 2 pencil point breaks, or the scan sheet rips...or God forbid both things happen! How do we help students as they are taking a test? The strategies and techniques in this section must be taught in the pre-testing phase; however, they are implemented by the test-taker in this phase. These strategies and techniques are more *student*-controlled than *teacher*-controlled. Whereas the teacher and parent have the greatest control is in the pre-testing phase, the student himself/herself is in charge once the test is in progress.

In this chapter, the following strategies and techniques are suggested as ways to assist students when they are in the process of taking a test:

- **Test-Taking Strategies**
- **Testing Modifications**
- **Techniques for Reducing Physical Symptoms**

- **Techniques for Reducing Emotional Symptoms**
- **Techniques for Reducing Mental/ Cognitive Symptoms**

If test-takers learn these strategies they will not only improve their odds of passing, but they will be more relaxed and focused in controlling their anxiety.

Test-Taking Strategies

Every test-taker needs to have strategies to handle the various types of items that are utilized on high stakes tests. We will examine several strategies for each test item type. These strategies will greatly increase the probability of getting the answer correct.

Multiple Choice Items

The popular game show, "Who Wants To Be A Millionaire?" is perhaps the best illustration of the use of multiple choice items. A *stem* is read either as an incomplete sentence or a question. For example:

"Christopher Columbus discovered America in _____."

or

"In which year did Christopher Columbus discover America?"

followed by a number of choices, usually four.

A. 1452	C. 1492
B. 1540	D. 1619.

The contestants are given three lifelines should they not know or are uncertain of their answer:

- 50/50
- Ask the Audience
- Phone-a-Friend

Each type of lifeline increases the probability that the contestants will choose the correct answer.

The 50/50 lifeline increases the probability of choosing the correct answer because the number of choices are reduced by taking away two wrong answers. Picking between two choices versus four makes a huge difference and greatly increases the odds of choosing the correct answer.

The Ask the Audience lifeline also increases the odds, because the majority or popular choice is more likely to be correct. Most contestants "play the odds" and go with the most popular choice as selected by the studio audience. But, of course, the most popular answer is not always the correct one.

The Phone-a-Friend lifeline increases the contestant's odds because they can call an individual who may be more knowledgeable about a certain topic. Unfortunately, preparing for high stakes tests is not like a game show.

Some refer to multiple choice as *multiple guess*. However, if you have studied well, multiple choice can be quite anxiety-lowering. After all, you are given the answer—all you need to do is find it among the choices. Although no lifeline exists when you take tests in school, utilizing some helpful but simple strategies can significantly increase your odds:

- **Begin by looking over the entire test before you start answering any questions.** How you manage your time on standardized tests is critical to your success. If you spend all of your time on the multiple choice part, you may not leave enough time to complete the other parts of the test such as the essay questions.

• **Underline or circle key words in the stem.**
Look for words that could significantly change the meaning, such as "most", "always", "some", "never", etc. Also, pay particular attention to any word that signals or denotes a negative.

"All of the following are minerals *except*..."
"Which triangle is *not* equilateral..."
"Identify the *least* effective means for reducing..."
"Which statement below is *incorrect*..."

Reading too quickly can easily cause the wrong answer to be selected. Circle or underline key words that can significantly change which answer is correct.

• **Increase your odds by trying to eliminate those choices that you believe to be incorrect.**
By reducing the number of choices (like 50/50), you will not be as overwhelmed when confronted with a difficult question. Sometimes, one choice provided is clearly wrong. For example:

"Who was the second President of the United States?"

    A. Thomas Jefferson   B. John Adams
    C. James Monroe   D. Abraham Lincoln

Obviously, you may not know who the second President was, but you may recognize that Lincoln was President at a much later time in our country's history.

    I strongly recommend that you literally cross off

any answers that you believe to be incorrect. Your odds of picking one correct answer out of two or three, versus picking one out of four or five, significantly improves your chances.

- **Answers that you first choose are often the best choices.** Don't assume every question is a trick question or an overly complicated one. Sometimes when we panic, we change our answer without clear justification other than our own nervousness. We think to ourselves, "It can't be that answer. That would be too easy." This phenomenon is especially true when a given test is particularly difficult. In such a situation where we do not know most of the answers, we get very nervous. So when we come upon a question that seems way too easy, instead of going with our first choice, we assume that it must be more complicated. Thus, we change our answer. Of course, if you reread the question and realize that you answered it wrong because you misunderstood it, then you should certainly change your answer.

- **Try to answer the easiest questions first and skip the more difficult ones.** This technique can be a very effective time saver. Imagine that the third multiple choice question in your test booklet is a very difficult one. You have no clue which of the four answers is correct. You spend several minutes dwelling on this item and increasing your anxiety as you realize that this is question number 3 out of 100! Skip it and move on. Come back to this question later, if you have time. Even if it is the type of test where guessing at an answer is better than not answering it, leave your guessing to the end.

- **Check periodically that you are aligning the computer answer sheet number correctly with the test questions.** Especially if you skip items, you must make sure that you are completing your answers to the correct test item on the bubble scoring sheet.

True/False Items

Although the odds of choosing the correct answer on a true/false item is 50/50, you will be surprised how anxiety can make such test items appear much more difficult than they really are. Here are some helpful tips:

- **Pick *true* unless you can prove that the statement is false.** This means that all parts of the statement must be true. For example:

> True or False: All Presidents of the United States lead the Executive Branch, serve as the Commander in Chief, and are elected.

Seems correct on the surface, but the answer is *false*. You could serve as President without being elected. Gerald Ford, after Richard Nixon's resignation, and Lyndon Baines Johnson, after Kennedy's assassination, are two examples of Presidents who were not elected. All parts of the statement must be *true* for the answer to be *true*.

- **Underline or circle key words**, especially such words as "not", "most", "always", "some", etc.

- **Watch out for absolute or qualified-type statements.** Usually, absolute types of statements are *false*. These are statements that use the words, "always", "all", "never", etc. For example:

True or False: A traumatic event always leads to post traumatic stress disorder.

Qualified-type statements, using words like "sometimes", "often", "on occasion" are usually *true*. For example:

True or False: Sometimes a traumatic event can lead to post traumatic stress disorder.

- **Unless the test penalizes for guessing, take a guess.** Your odds of getting the answer right are much better with True/False than with multiple choice. So it is foolish not to guess. However, remember that all guesses should be "educated" ones, not random ones.

Matching and Fill-in-the-Blank Items

When taking high stakes exams, there exist other types of test items which can pose difficulty for the test anxious student as well. Two types of questions that are commonly used, although significantly less than multiple choice, are *matching* and *fill-in-the-blank*. At first glance, matching items appears to be easier since, like multiple choice, the test-taker is given options. Fill-in-the-blank, however, does not provide any choices. Nevertheless, when under stress, there are valuable strategies that can be employed. The following are examples based on material that was covered in Chapter 3:

Find the "parenting type" in Column A that best matches each statement listed in Column B.

Column A

1. The Critic
2. The Worrier
3. The Perfectionist
4. The Victim

Column B

_____ "It's not your fault that you failed the test."

_____ "You passed, but you should have scored much higher."

_____ "What if you fail the test again?"

_____ "I heard that your friend did better than you."

In order to be successful on *matching* items, many of the same points apply as with multiple choice and 50/50 test items:

- **Read the items and statements carefully.**

- **Match the easiest items first.**

- **Look for key words or concepts** that might help separate one choice from another. For example, distinguishing between The Critic and The Perfectionist is harder than distinguishing between the other types. Therefore, notice that "should have" was in one statement. Recall that "shoulds" are to The Perfectionist as "what if's" are to The Worrier. So, "should" is a key word. Also, one statement made a comparison to someone else. Remember, The Critic often uses putdowns and compares his/her child negatively to others.

- **Guessing when you only have several matches left** is the best last resort.

Similarly, *fill-in-the-blank* questions are basically the stem of a multiple choice question without the choices. In addition to the points made above about reading carefully, completing easy answers (matches) first, and looking for key words, you should:

- **Consider the grammar of the sentence.** Sometimes the word to be completed is a descriptor. Other times, it is a proper name. For example:

Fear is our response to a _____ danger.

Anxiety is our response to a _____ danger.

Two domains that contribute to test anxiety are:

    1) an individual's characteristics and

    2) the_____ in which they live, work and play.

- **Think and use logic.** If you reread the sentence and it does not make sense, then choose a different word.

Essay-Type Items

This category of test items incorporates written short answers as well as longer, more traditional essay questions. We can divide our test-taking strategies into two parts:

- strategies to better understand the questions posed

- strategies to better organize and write responses.

We must begin with the question. For example, if you were to write an essay about one of the stakeholder groups that contributes to test anxiety, the question might be as follows:

Essay Question:	Describe how classroom teachers contribute to raising the levels of test anxiety. Identify two specific ways that they can help lower test anxiety in their students.

In order to effectively answer this question, it needs to be dissected. It has two parts, and it asks two different, but related things. It asks the test-taker to:

• describe   and   • identify

Read each question focusing on key words. Words that are often used in essay questions that help us fashion our response include:

discuss	describe
define	summarize
compare	contrast
identify	list
explain	outline
evaluate	provide or support (a position)
prove	defend or refute (a position)
illustrate	give an opinion

You need to know what is expected of you before you can answer the essay question. And, like all other test items, key words are significant to identify and underline (or circle). When words like "discuss", "describe", or "explain" are used, the answer must be based on providing general information in a logical and organized fashion.

When words like "identify" or "list" are used, the answer calls for more specific information often containing a series of items to be presented. So we must begin by understanding clearly what we need to do.

Strategies for organizing and writing essays successfully can be categorized as follows:

- **Use an outline and identify your main points**, especially if the essay needs to be long. Use those main points to develop your paragraphs.

- **Use a graphic organizer** or other type of visual framework to assist you to lay out your written response.

- **Open and close your essay by relating directly to what you are asked to do.** Namely, your first and last paragraphs should make it clear to the reader what your purpose is. If you are comparing and contrasting forms of government, then the first paragraph should set the stage and your last paragraph should summarize or conclude your main points.

- **Use references and research to back up your writing**, especially when you are asked to "defend", "evaluate", "support", or "refute" a position or statement. As part of your preparation and study skills, you hopefully will be aware of the essay questions that are normally asked and you would have taken a practice test or two.

- **Be sensitive to the technical aspects of writing** including sentence structure, grammar, spelling and punctuation. Although test scorers are very concerned with the content of your response, mechanical aspects are also be very important.

Chart XXII
Helpful Test-Taking Strategies

For Multiple Choice Items

- Look over the entire exam before you start.
- Underline or circle key words that could change meaning (i.e. not, except, least, never, etc.).
- Eliminate choices that you know are incorrect first.
- Stick with your first answer if in doubt.
- Answer easier items first.
- Periodically check alignment of the answer sheet with the proper question.

For True/False Items

- Pick "True" unless you can prove otherwise (all parts must be "True").
- Underline or circle key words.
- Be careful of both "absolute" and "qualified-type" statements.
- Guess unless penalized for doing so.

For Matching/Fill-in-the-Blank Items

- Read items very carefully.
- Match/complete easiest items first.
- Look for key words and concepts.
- Guess when only several matches are left.
- Look at grammar/sentence structure.
- Think carefully using logic.

For Essay-Type Items

- Read question carefully focusing on key words (i.e. "describe", "define", "list", "compare", "contrast", "evaluate", etc.).
- Use an outline and identify main points.
- Use a graphic organizer.
- Open and close the essay by focusing on the purpose.
- Use references and resources to support key points.
- Be sensitive to technical aspects of writing (i.e., sentence structure, grammar, spelling and punctuation).
- Proofread if time allows.
- Be conscious of time.
- Write clearly and legibly.

- **Be conscious of time.** If you know that you write slowly, then allow more time to finish the essay. That is why I recommended earlier to look over the entire test before starting to answer any questions. If there are two essays versus one, that could greatly change how you allocate and manage the time spent on each section of the exam.

- **Write as clearly and as legibly as you can**. If a scorer cannot read what you have written, it will definitely lower your score. You probably will not have time to rewrite or recopy your work. So the use of an outline becomes that much more important.

- **Always proofread your work if time allows.**

Testing Modifications

If a student has a disability, either under the Individuals with Disabilities Education Act (IDEA), or under Section 504 of the Rehabilitation Act, he or she may be entitled to testing modifications, sometimes referred to as non-standardized test administration.

These testing modifications are designed to greatly reduce the negative impact of the disability during the test-taking experience, as well as to reduce the associated anxiety. The testing modifications provided must be absolutely necessary, and must be written into either a student's Individual Education Program (IEP) under IDEA, or in an Accommodation Plan under Section 504. Testing modifications can be categorized into four basic types:

- **Access Accommodations** - provide the student with access to devices or materials that he/she might not otherwise have access to. (For example, a word processor, calculator, spell checker, arithmetic tables, manipulatives, etc.)

- **Time Accommodations** - adjust the length or scheduling of the test. (For example, extended time or flexible scheduling allowing the test to be taken in smaller units.)

- **Location Accommodations** - allow a student to take the test in a separate location or with a smaller group.

- **Administration Accommodations** - change or alter how the test is administered. (For example, reading the directions or parts of the test to a student, or allowing the elimination of certain requirements such as correct punctuation or spelling.)

It must be emphasized that only a deserving student with a disability should receive a testing modification, and only the specific type of accommodation needed for that type of disability should be provided.

I encourage all parents of children with suspected or identified disabilities to contact the appropriate officials in their school district to further explore their child's rights to testing modifications. However, they should not try to manipulate the system by requesting testing modifications that are truly not appropriate.

Recently, there has been increasing pressure to limit or reduce the availability of testing modifications. As the use of high stakes tests have expanded, so has the number of students receiving testing modifications. Cognizant of that fact, some state education departments are placing limitations on which types of modifications will be allowed for certain tests.

Chart XXIII

Testing Modifications

Type	Examples	For Use With
Access	• Access to spell check • Access to tape recorder • Use of calculator • Use of arithmetic tables • Use of manipulatives for computation • Use of "scribe" • Access to computer/word Processor	Disabilities related to assessed discrepancies in writing/spelling mechanics, visual or graphomotor skills, memory, math processing, etc.
Time	• Extended time • Flexible scheduling (including use of breaks)	Disabilities related to "processing" time, certain medical conditions, attentional disorders, etc.
Location	• Separate location • Small group administration • One-on-one administration	Disabilities related to distractibility, or needed to deliver other types of modifications (e.g., use of scribe)
Administration	• Directions read (or re-read) • Questions read (or re-read) • Eliminate requirements (e.g., spelling or punctuation) • Provide additional directions or explanation	Disabilities related to reading/language, writing, attentional disorders, etc.

△ Techniques to Reduce Anxiety Symptoms

Based on The Test Anxiety Triangle presented in Chapter 4, we are now going to review effective techniques that lower anxiety during the time frame just before and during the test administration itself. Remember that these techniques must be taught and practiced during the pre-testing phase to be effective. Furthermore, each technique, although categorized by type of symptom (physical, emotional and mental) is helpful at reducing the *overall* feeling of anxiety. As explained in Chapter 4, anxiety involves physiological, emotional, and cognitive processing. The impact of one technique targeted at a particular type of symptom, therefore influences all three components.

△ Techniques to Reduce Physical Symptoms

Clearly the best approach for reducing the physical symptoms of test anxiety is to learn how to relax. However, that is much easier said than done. In fact, the more people are told to relax in anxious situations, often the more anxious they become. It is difficult for students to learn how to relax, but there are techniques that can be taught so that they can control their own physical reactions during the exam. Learning to relax and calm one's self down is a critical component to success on any type of test. The following techniques can dramatically reduce the physical symptoms of test anxiety:

- **Deep Breathing**
- **Progressive Muscle Relaxation**
- **Physical Exercise**

Remember, these techniques need to be taught and practiced in the pre-testing phase to be successful.

Chart XXIV

Techniques to Reduce
Test Anxiety Symptoms (Summary)

	Symptoms	Techniques
△ Physical Component	- Body temperature changes - Breathing difficulties - Muscular stiffness - Abdominal complaints - Cardiovascular problems	- Deep breathing - Progressive muscle relaxation - Physical exercise
△ Emotional Component	- Mood changes - Emotionality - Fears of loss of control	- Visualization - Meditation - Self-Expression
△ Mental/Cognitive Component	- Irrational thinking - Feelings of failure or rejection - Memory loss - Loss of concentration	- Positive self-talk

Deep Breathing

Sometimes called abdominal breathing, deep breathing helps to increase the supply of oxygen to the body and leads to greater relaxation. When we are in a stressful situation, our breathing becomes short and shallow, which can lead to hyperventilation. When we hyperventilate, we breath out too much carbon dioxide relative to the amount of oxygen in our blood stream. This lack of carbon dioxide in the blood often leads to a harder and faster heart rate. Hyperventilation can also lead to constriction of blood vessels in the brain which can cause feelings of dizziness or light-headedness.

The old cure for hyperventilation is breathing into a paper bag because it causes you to breathe in more carbon dioxide restoring the balance of carbon dioxide and oxygen in your blood. Now, I'm not suggesting that you bring a paper bag with your sharpened No. 2 pencils to the exam, but I am, however, suggesting that you learn some breathing exercises.

Step 1:   Get in a relaxed position. A seated position with both feet on the floor is best and most practical since you will be using this technique during a test.

Step 2:   Begin by inhaling slowly and deeply through your nose. Try to breathe from your abdomen up. Some people suggest that placing a hand on your abdomen under your rib cage is helpful. As you breathe deeply, your hand will rise as your abdominal muscles expand. Your chest should not move very much. (To note the difference between abdominal breathing and shallower breathing, try to breathe in and out of your mouth. You will notice that in this type of shallower breathing your chest moves up and down considerably.)

Step 3:   After you have taken a deep breath, hold it for a second or two and exhale slowly through your nose or mouth. As you exhale, try to let your body relax and go limp. Closing your eyes as you inhale and exhale can help greatly.

Step 4: Keep your breathing slow and smooth. Keep a rhythm. Some people like to count in their heads to establish a regular pattern. Take at least five full abdominal breaths. If you feel dizzy or light-headed, stop for a minute or so, and then begin again.

Step 5: Ideally, breathing for three to five minutes is desirable. You may also choose to hold your exhales a bit longer before each inhale. However, your concerns about time may not permit it. Since virtually all high stakes tests are timed, the anxiety about spending too much time on breathing can lead to even more anxiety. So keep it short.

The most important thing about abdominal breathing is to concentrate on your breathing. Clear your mind, and keep your body as relaxed as possible.

Progressive Muscle Relaxation

Another effective technique for reducing physical symptoms associated with test anxiety is called progressive muscle relaxation. More than 50 years ago, Dr. Edmund Jacobson, in a book called *Progressive Relaxation*, developed exercises that relax the muscle by first tensing it. There have been many variations of muscle relaxation exercises over the years. I am proposing a simple progressive pattern working from your toes and feet all the way up the body to your forehead.

Step 1: Get in a relaxed position. Once again, upright in a chair with your feet flat on the floor and your lower back firmly against the back of the chair is ideal. Close your eyes.

Step 2: Tighten your feet by curling your toes in. Hold for 5 - 10 seconds, then release for 10 - 15 seconds. Repeat two or three times. Focus on how relaxed your feet feel after you release the tension.

Step 3: Tighten your calf muscles. Hold for 5 - 10 seconds, then release for 10 - 15 seconds. Once again, depending on time, you can repeat tightening and releasing two or three times.

Step 4: Tighten your thigh muscles. Hold for 5 - 10 seconds, then release for 10 - 15 seconds. Again, repeat two or three times if possible.

Step 5: Tighten your buttocks by pulling them together. Hold for 5 - 10 seconds, then release for 10 - 15 seconds. Repeat two or three times if possible.

Step 6: Tighten your stomach muscles by sucking in your stomach. Hold in your stomach for 5 - 10 seconds, then release it for 10 - 15 seconds. Repeat two or three times as indicated in the earlier steps.

Step 7: Tighten your chest by taking a deep breath in through your mouth. Hold it for 5 - 10 seconds, then release for 10 - 15 seconds. Repeat two or three times.

Step 8: Tighten your fists by clenching them. Hold them for 5 - 10 seconds, then release for 10 - 15 seconds. Repeat two or three times.

Step 9:   Tense your arms by flexing your biceps. Hold for 5 - 10 seconds, then release for 10 - 15 seconds. Repeat two or three times.

Step 10:   Tighten your shoulders by pulling them back as far as you can. Hold for 5 - 10 seconds, then release for 10 - 15 seconds. Repeat two or three times.

Step 11:   Tighten your neck by moving it back and aiming your chin toward the ceiling. Hold it for 5 - 10 seconds, then release for 10 - 15 seconds. Repeat two or three times.

Step 12:   Tighten your face muscles by raising or lowering your eyebrows (whichever is most effective for you). Hold for 5 - 10 seconds, then release for 10 - 15 seconds. Repeat two or three times.

You may also tighten and loosen other muscle groups such as your jaw or back muscles. Some people prefer to focus only on certain muscle groups, targeting where they are most stressed. Whatever you choose, make sure that it is effective and that you relax the entire body once a specific muscle group is released.

Physical Exercise

It has been widely documented by medical research that exercise can relieve stress. However, there are no state-mandated or other high stakes tests that will allow students to stop in the middle and do physical exercises. Could you imagine getting up from your seat and doing Tae Bo? If you cannot leave the exam room even to take a short walk, then why am I listing physical exercise as a technique to reduce test anxiety?

Because physical exercise can help students relax during the days leading up to the test, including the morning of the test. Also, some tests are given over multiple sessions with breaks in between, and over multiple days. The benefits of exercise to counteract the physical symptoms of anxiety are truly outstanding. More oxygen in the blood to improve circulation and the release of any pent up tension are only a few of the many advantages of exercise.

Please note: obtain the advice of your physician or other health care provider before starting any regimen.

The exercises that are best for students who are anxious about tests (as well as during test preparation and study) include:

Aerobic exercise - Any exercise that increases cardiovascular functioning is great, such as walking, jogging, running, jumping rope, stair climbing, cycling, and the like. As always, it is advised that you should warm up and stretch first. The long term benefits to your health in terms of weight control, reducing heart disease and improving overall health are clear, but a sustained regular pattern of exercise must be followed. Exercise is a great way to address test anxiety because it is simple to do and has the added benefit of providing relaxation. It also takes your mind off of your worries and redirects your energies. Whenever you are tired of studying or stressed from working too long, a brief walk, even if it is only around your school or home, can truly make a difference.

Stretching exercises - Have you ever travelled a long distance sitting in one position? For example, driving a car for several hours on a highway and then stopping at a rest area. What did it feel like to stretch? It probably felt terrific, because our bodies are not programmed to stay in one position too long. So during what could be a two or three hour test, you need to stretch. Once again, standing and doing abdominal and leg exercises in the middle of the examination room would not be too popular with the proctor. In fact, that may be the best way to quickly end the test for you, since you will be escorted out.

However, you can do a series of stretching exercises in your seat. Examples include:

- Extending each of your legs straight out in front of you and raising them off the floor a few inches.

- Moving your feet back and forth at the ankles.

- Stretching each of your arms out in front of you or out to the side.

- Circling your head using your neck or moving your head from side to side (or from front to back). Move your chin down to your chest and then point your chin to ceiling.

- Moving your shoulders up and down or back and forth.

- Repositioning yourself in your seat can also help alleviate fatigue and improve feeling in your body (especially your back).

When you take tests you are often sitting on hard (unpadded) chairs at a desk or table, so you must recognize that body movement is important and be prepared to stretch at least every 20-30 minutes.

Nutrition, as well as exercise, can play a significant role in reducing physical symptoms, and some helpful information is listed in Appendix B.

△ Techniques to Reduce Emotional Symptoms

The following techniques are useful in reducing the emotional symptoms of test anxiety:

- **Visualization**
- **Meditation**
- **Self-Expression**

As stated with the strategies presented earlier, these techniques need to be learned and practiced in the pre-testing phase in order to be effective.

Visualization

A very effective way to reduce the emotional symptoms associated with anxiety is the process of visualization. This is the technique of closing your eyes and imagining a calm, peaceful scene whenever you are beginning to feel anxious. Sometimes it is a scene that is based on a past pleasant experience, such as a trip to the beach, a park or other special place. Or, it could be a scene that you have never experienced but wish to.

It's best that the individual identifies his/her own scene for the visualization rather than being given one by someone else. Effective visualization scenes include the following criteria:

- peaceful and calm
- multisensory - using as many of the senses as possible
- able to generate pleasant and happy feelings (the thought itself can bring a smile to your face)
- based on the individual's personal experience
- places where the individual would like to travel

For me, a good visualization would be a scene where I'm lying on a beach feeling the warm rays of the sun on my skin and a soft breeze against my face. I would hear the waves of the ocean breaking on the shore, and the sounds of seagulls in the distance. I could literally smell the salt water. A peacefulness and calmness would come over me. Notice that each of the above criteria was met by this visualization

---

The Park Scene

Imagine sitting under a large oak tree on a crisp autumn morning. The colorful leaves gently falling down around you. Off in the distance you see a crystal clear pond with a beautiful swan peacefully gliding across the still water. The water is like a mirror reflecting the deep blue sky. You hear the faint laughter of children in the distance. All is well with the world.

The Golf Course Scene

Picture yourself standing on an elevated tee of a magnificent golf hole looking down to the beautifully manicured green, surrounded by traps that look like small white sandy beaches. Large evergreens line both sides of the fairway like green picket fences. The flag is gently blowing in the wind. You can smell the freshly cut grass, and all you can hear are birds chirping in the trees. It is a peaceful and tranquil feeling.

The Garden Scene

You can feel and smell the freshly tilled moist soil in your hands as you plant some new seeds in the flower garden. The sun has just risen in the sky and the air is crisp and clean. The smell of flowers that have already bloomed fills the air. A monarch butterfly lands on a flower and you admire its color and beauty. You and nature are as one.

The Sailboat Scene

Imagine lying on the deck of a beautiful sailboat being steadily pushed by the wind at sea. You look up at the large mast and extended sail and breathe in the fresh salt air. You feel the warm sun on your clothes and feel a slight mist from the ocean's water. The only sound is the waves against the boat as it gracefully moves through the dark blue water. The movement is smooth and in rhythm. You are one with the sea.

scene. Other sample visualization scenes could include:

As I wrote these scenes, I literally began to visualize them. The reason is that I have experienced each of these scenes in my lifetime. They are all wonderful memories imprinted in my mind. Just writing these scenes relaxed me, and I forgot about my publisher's deadline and all of the other pressures associated with finishing this book.

Believe me, using visualization when you are in anxiety provoking situations is a powerful way to get your emotional symptoms under control. Although children do not have as much experience in their lives to draw from because of their younger ages, they can be very effective in using visualizations.

First, many children and adolescents have vivid fantasy lives and active imaginations. They are likely to create or recreate scenes from a movie or dream that they have experienced. Kids can transport themselves more readily in their minds than adults, who may be more reticent about using visualization. Some adults think that if kids use visualization, that they are daydreaming. Call it what you want. If it helps to lower anxiety and improve test scores, then it should be used.

Second, children and adolescents will find this technique fun-filled. They will try to imagine scenes from sports or other social situations that they will want repeated in their lives again and again. Of course returning from the peaceful scene, opening your eyes and staring at a chemistry test in front of you can be problematic. Therefore, at the end of the visualization, which I recommend be no more than a minute or two, you should count to five before opening your eyes. If you are still very anxious, then return to the visualization again for a short time. When you feel that you are calmer, return back to the test.

Meditation

The use of meditation as a means to calm one's self and be at peace is thousands of years old. It was not until the 1960's that our western culture began to accept meditation as a viable practice. Transcendental meditation (TM), where an instructor identifies a mantra (a word or sound) for an individual to focus on and repeat, was the most common form used for many years. Meditation is not like visualization, in that meditation should be practiced every day, even for a few minutes. Also, meditation is more of a preventive technique than visualization, which is a reactionary technique. In other words, you don't practice meditation to cope with a panic attack, you practice meditation so you do not have panic attacks.

In *The Relaxation Response*, Herbert Benson developed his own version of meditation which produced significant positive psychological results, such as lowered heart rate and blood pressure, as well as decreased oxygen consumption and metabolic rate. Benson's method was based on breathing and not on an individually selected mantra. In fact, Benson developed a version where a person would mentally repeat the word "one" with each exhalation of breath.

Edmund Bourne in his best selling book, *The Anxiety and Phobia Workbook* lists two types of meditation:

1. **Using a mantra** (selecting a word/phrase or Sanskrit mantra such as "Om Shanti", "Sri Ram", and "So-Hum"). Repeat this word/phrase on each exhalation. As thoughts come to your mind, let them go and bring your attention back to the repetitive word or phrase.

2. **Counting breaths.** Focus on the inflow and outflow of your breath and count as you breathe out. As thoughts come to mind or your focus wanders, go back to your breathing and counting. If you lose track of your count, start back at one or a round number. Eventually you can stop counting and focus solely on your breathing.

Regardless of the type of meditation used, Bourne provides a series of guidelines for practicing meditation which can be summarized as follows:

• **Find a quiet environment and reduce noise.** If

that is not possible, play soft instrumental sounds or sounds from nature, like ocean waves breaking on the shore.

- **Reduce muscle tension**—use progressive muscle relaxation.

- **Sit properly**—Eastern style: sit cross-legged on a pillow placed on the floor, and rest your hands on your thighs. Western style: sit in a comfortable chair with feet flat on the floor. In either position, keep your back and neck straight without straining to do so.

- **Set aside 20 - 30 minutes for meditation.** Beginners may wish to start out with a smaller period of time such as 5 - 10 minutes. Use a timer or play background music or sounds that are the desired length so that you will know when you are done.

- **Make it a regular practice to meditate every day.** Find a set time to practice meditating.

- **Don't meditate on a full stomach or when you are tired.**

- **Select a focus for your attention.** Either a mantra or on your breathing, as described earlier.

- **Assume a non-judgemental passive attitude.** This means concentrate, and when your attention wanders from your mantra or breathing, gently bring it back again. Understand that distractions are normal. Do not dwell on the outcome of your meditation. The more you let go, the deeper your experience of the meditation will be.

There are many books on the market regarding meditation. I recommend that those interested in using meditation as a technique to reduce test anxiety go to their library and read several books on the subject.

Self-Expression

Perhaps one of the easiest and best techniques to reduce the negative effects of the emotional symptoms of test anxiety is expressing your feelings (self-expression). It is easiest in terms of technique, but perhaps the hardest in terms of action.

Many of us have increased anxiety because we have been unable to express and/or channel our feelings in productive ways. In other words, we hold our feelings in and we do not readily seek out others to share our fears and concerns. These inner fears we carry with us like baggage.

In fact, that is why therapy can be so successful. It isn't necessarily that the therapist possesses such unique skills of insight, although many do. It is that the patient seeks out help and opens up about their emotional problem.

It is often said that it is impossible to help a person who is seriously alcohol or drug dependent until that person is out of the denial stage. In other words, rehabilitation is not likely to succeed unless a person recognizes his/her problems and desires to come to grips with them. The same is true for the test-anxious individual. If he or she is not able to acknowledge the need for help, then reducing anxiety is not likely to occur. Fortunately, most anxious people feel uncomfortable about their condition and are more likely to seek help.

The first step in seeking help is a willingness to come forward and express it in words—to tell a teacher, parent or friend that one is anxious about a test and that it is interfering with the ability to study and prepare. Often times, kids' feelings of rejection get in the way of coming forward. They may be fearful that others will make fun of them or think less of them if they truly express their anxious feelings. That is why we must help them open the door and "unpack the baggage."

One of the most powerful things we can do for children and adolescents is create an environment that says "we love you no matter what happens." Carl Rogers used to call this *unconditional positive regard.* If kids feel safe in expressing their feelings, they will be more apt to do so. Then, we can help them understand that:

- many of these feelings are normal
- many other kids feel just as they do
- most importantly, they can get help and support in reducing test anxiety

Since our goal is to raise awareness of test anxiety as an issue, schools need to "step up to the plate." Schools, as organizations, are in the best position to create environments for increased awareness and self-expression for students as a part of their test preparation efforts. Remember, many students are test anxious to varying degrees, so the efforts made by school staff will be well worth it. Over time, students will become better test-takers resulting in higher test scores. This fact not only benefits students. In many school districts, higher test scores will yield increased funding, so the investment is definitely worth the effort. How can schools afford not to formalize their efforts?

There are many ways for schools to nurture an environment for open self-expression. Chart XXV lists a few options. Remember that self-expression begins with *self-awareness.* Unless students recognize the symptoms they feel, they will not be able to take the next step to communicate them to others. In chapters 7 and 8, we discuss how goal setting and planning are important strategies to turn self-expression into *self-help.*

Chart XXV

Ways Schools Can Increase Self-Expression (Relating to Test Anxiety)

- Create a "Drop In" Center for students.
- Establish a confidential "sign-up" system for students interested in talking about upcoming tests.
- Provide self-assessment surveys regarding test anxiety that students can complete.
- Offer a "Strategies to Reduce Test Anxiety" seminar after school or on Saturday mornings (one for staff and one for students).
- Incorporate discussions on test anxiety into all school/ classroom test preparation initiatives.
- Ensure that all staff (especially mental health professionals) are trained to identify the symptoms of test anxiety and implement strategies to reduce them.
- Send a flyer home to parents encouraging them to inform the school if their child is anxious and needs support. (It could also contain some helpful tips for parents.)
- Expand the school's web site to include commonly asked questions and answers. (Institute an e-mail component for parents and students to communicate.)
- Establish a telephone hot-line during prescribed hours for students or parents to call before an upcoming test.

Teacher as Therapist

I'm not really proposing that teachers become therapists. After all, that is a profession that requires much
specialized training. Teachers choose education as a career
because they want to teach, not because they want to
conduct psychoanalysis. But I have been in education for
nearly 30 years, and it has been my experience that the best
teachers are also therapists.

By that I mean, they listen to their students. They
communicate to them that they care about their well being
and, most importantly, they support their students by taking
action to help them become good, successful human beings.
The teacher as therapist metaphor fits like a glove.

Students communicate their anxieties to their teacher
in the following ways:

1. talking about their feelings

2. writing about their feelings.

Obviously, students can and do also communicate their
anxiety by their behavior. But I would argue that teaching
them to unpack their baggage through verbal or written
expression is the best way to help them. Waiting until a
student falls apart in class on the day of a test is not the
most teachable moment.

Teachers and parents must create environments in
their classrooms and homes that nurture either or both of
these communication approaches. One non-threatening
approach to get kids to talk in school is through the use of
surveys or questionnaires as an entry point.

Using Surveys or Questionnaires

Teachers often ask, "Where do I begin?" "Do I just
get up in front of the class and ask: Who's afraid to take next

month's math test? Please raise your hand." Of course not. Teachers can give their students a simple survey or question-naire that asks some basic questions about test anxiety (refer to samples on pages that follow).

Surveys, of course, should be tailored to the age and reading level of the students, and can be completed anony-mously. The teacher collects them and tallys the results. The results may then be shared in class, with the teacher encouraging classroom participation. Remember to preface whatever students say about anxiety in class with com-ments about listening and respecting others' points of view.

Creating positive environments can occur on a schoolwide basis with assemblies on test anxiety and prepara-tion, at grade level meetings, or working in individual classes. Bringing targeted students together to talk is probably the most effective group situation for expression. For example, providing opportunities for special education students or students with Section 504 accommodation plans, or ELL (English Language Learner) students to discuss their feelings and anxieties might be quite helpful.

Obviously one method doesn't preclude the other. A large class lesson does not prevent the teacher from also targeting specific students whom he/she knows are more likely to be test-anxious. Many teachers feel that targeted small group lessons or one-on-one discussions are the best interventions when dealing with something as personal as test anxiety. However, merely asking about test anxiety, even discussing its symptoms, is inadequate. It could even raise some kids' anxiety even more. The discussions must be coupled with a plan to teach techniques to help kids take control. We want kids to express and talk about test anxiety as a prelude to doing something about it.

Chart XXVI

Sample Student Survey

"All About Tests"

1) When I am told by my teacher that an important test is coming up, I feel_____

2) I study for most tests by _____
_____
_____

3) I sometimes worry about _____
_____
_____

4) The night before the test I _____
_____
_____

5) On the day of the test I try to _____
_____
_____

6) As I am taking an important test, I feel _____
_____
_____

7) After a test is over, I usually feel _____

Chart XXVII
Sample Test Anxiety Questionnaire

	Never	Sometimes	Always
1. I become nervous several days before I have to take an important test.	☐	☐	☐
2. I cannot sleep the night before a test.	☐	☐	☐
3. I cannot eat the morning of an important test.	☐	☐	☐
4. My palms sweat, my stomach has butterflies, or I have other similar symptoms when the test is being handed out or distributed.	☐	☐	☐
5. I cannot focus or concentrate when I first open the test booklet.	☐	☐	☐
6. I have to read and re-read the directions many times.	☐	☐	☐
7. I feel light-headed or like I'm going to pass out during the test.	☐	☐	☐
8. I cannot concentrate or focus during the test.	☐	☐	☐
9. My mind goes blank during the test.	☐	☐	☐
10. Negative thoughts enter my mind during the test.	☐	☐	☐
11. I change my answers many times.	☐	☐	☐
12. I constantly worry about what time it is and how much time I have left.	☐	☐	☐
13. During the test, I feel like I'm going to have a panic attack.	☐	☐	☐
14. After the test, I am totally exhausted.	☐	☐	☐
15. After the test, I usually think I have failed.	☐	☐	☐

Chart XXVIII

Positive Environments for Self-Expression

Environment	Options		
In the Classroom	Whole class discussion	Small group dialogue	One-on-one discussion
In the School	School-wide assembly	Grade level meeting	Targeted group meeting
In the Home	Family discussion	Parent/child discussion	Older sibling to younger sibling discussion

Mental Health Professionals

Using school psychologists, social workers, or guidance counselors to conduct small groups should be part of a school's repertoire of effective strategies. These trained mental health professionals in schools are skilled in counseling techniques and in giving the necessary emotional support to kids with excessive stress.

Schools should establish test anxiety and preparation drop-in centers where kids can go on their free time to talk and seek help. A location with set hours of operation is desirable. Psychologists, social workers or guidance counselors might also establish a system where kids could confidentially sign up to talk with someone. Based on this initial meeting, the student and the school mental health professional could jointly develop a plan of action. The student could be offered to be included as part of an existing group that is discussing test anxiety, or the student could agree to have the mental health professional contact his or her teacher or parents to help them work together on a collaborative plan. The options are endless. More specific information on developing plans to reduce test anxiety is covered in Chapter 8.

Chart XXIX

Human Resources Available to Students

School Resources

- General education classroom teachers
- Special education teachers
- Health teachers
- School psychologists
- School social workers
- Guidance counselors
- School nurses
- Speech/language therapists
- Principals and assistant principals

Home and Community Resources

- Parents
- Older siblings
- Close friends/relatives
- Mental health workers
- Private therapists
- Test preparation centers

We must begin with expanding the opportunities for student self-expression. Students must have places to go to talk about what is bothering them. As for expressing their concerns in writing beyond completing surveys or question-naires, students could be encouraged to submit their con-cerns in writing to their teacher or school mental health worker. A mailbox or e-mail at the drop-in center could be established for students who prefer writing over talking. As stated earlier, classroom teachers could provide simple open-ended surveys where students could express their feelings in writing, particularly if they are uncomfortable talking about this issue in front of the whole class or even in a small group.

Parent as Therapist

It is estimated that between eight and ten percent of all American children and adolescents suffer from serious anxiety. Millions are psychiatrically diagnosed with an anxi-ety disorder such as obsessive-compulsive disorder, or gener-alized anxiety disorder. For many of these children and adolescents, test anxiety is only a small part of dealing with a life full of apprehension and worry. Although professional help needs to be sought out, parents can play a very positive role in alleviating anxiety in their children.

In their book, *Your Anxious Child*, John Dacey and Lisa Fiore present the COPE Method. This approach was initially designed to help students improve their study habits and decrease use of drugs, and later it was adapted specifi-cally to help students with anxiety problems. Their book is filled with practical strategies that address each of the four steps in COPE. Although Dacey and Fiore do not focus specifically on test anxiety, many of the techniques they present can be adapted by parents for use with their test-anxious children. The more skilled parents become at helping their children reduce anxiety, the more effective and positive the results. The first way for parents to become more skilled is through increasing their own knowledge. In the Bibliography there are a number of books that can help parents better understand and address anxiety in their children.

Chart XXX

The COPE Method*

C = **Calming the Nervous System**
The need to address the physiological symptoms associated with anxiety.

O = **Originating an Imaginative Plan**
The need to develop creative ideas and effective problem solving.

P = **Persisting in the Face of Obstacles and Failures**
The need to persevere in the face of adversity by having faith in oneself.

E = **Evaluating and Adjusting the Plan**
The need to get objective feedback on how the plan is working.

* Content from *Your Anxious Child* by John Dacey and Lisa Fiore

---

Techniques to Reduce Mental/Cognitive Symptoms

Remember, the irrational thinking and faulty logic that so often accompany test anxiety can increase the test-taker's stress levels and significantly reduce his/her memory and concentration during the test. It is best to combat negative logic with positive logic.

Positive Self-Talk

The best strategy to counteract the cognitive symptoms of anxiety, like irrational thinking and feelings of failure and rejection, is positive self-talk. Self-talk is the process of saying statements to or having a conversation with oneself. It is literally the things that we say in our heads that effect our thinking, our feelings and our mood. Sometimes we talk to ourselves out loud, but self-talk is usually a silent, internally-driven mental process. Self-talk is the cognitive/mental part of test anxiety and it can have a positive or negative impact on our behavior. Simply put, we need to move from "what if..." thinking to "so what..." thinking, or to "I can handle it..." thinking. The faulty beliefs listed in Chart XXXI illustrate the differences between negative self-talk and positive self-talk. The key to using positive self-talk techniques is to first recognize what you are saying to yourself—write it down and counteract the faulty or mistaken belief with a positive (but true) statement. As you read the negative self-talk statements, note that they come from a variety of faulty beliefs based on feelings of failure, rejection or loss of control. Basically, we as individuals intellectualize our feelings by putting them into words. These words can send powerful messages that influence behavior.

Chart XXXI

Self-Talk Statements

Negative Self-Talk Statements	Positive Self-Talk Statements
(Based on faulty beliefs)	(What I should be saying to myself)
What if I fail? Everyone will think I'm stupid.	I am intelligent. Failing is OK. My worth as a person is not based on my performance on one test.
What if I fail? My parents, teachers and friends will think less of me.	My parents and teachers love me. True friends care about me regardless how I perform on the test.
What if I fail again? Because I failed my English test last semester, I am likely to fail again.	Just because I failed before doesn't mean I will fail again. I will study more/differently and prepare better this time.
What if I do not score high? I should be able to answer every question.	No one is perfect. I will prepare and do my best.
What if the test covers the course content that I least understand? I can't control what is on the test, so I am really powerless in preparing.	I can handle it. I am in control. I will study content I am least comfortable with harder and more carefully.
I am poor at math, so I know I will certainly fail.	Because I am not as good in math as I am in my other subjects, I need to work harder to prepare.

continued...

...continued

Negative Self-Talk Statements
(Based on faulty beliefs)

Positive Self-Talk Statements
(What I should be saying to myself)

What if I told others that I am worried about the test? People would laugh and ridicule me.

Many people get anxious about tests and other important things. I should not be afraid to share my feelings.

If I worry a lot about the upcoming test, I will be motivated and prepare better.

Worrying will not help me pass any test. Preparation will.

What if I freeze during the test? What if I get nervous and forget everything I've learned?

I can handle it. I will use the relaxation techniques that I have learned to reduce my anxiety.

I don't know what I will do if my SAT scores are low. I will not get into a top college.

I will take an SAT preparation course and prepare the best I can. Worrying about it won't help me. I will talk to my guidance counselor about colleges. I will take the ACT as well.

If I fail this admission exam, my life is over. I really must get into this private school.

No way is my life over. If I fail I will be disappointed, but life will go on.

Tips for Classroom Use

As with the techniques identified throughout this chapter, a teacher can develop several short lessons on self-talk as follows:

<u>Step 1</u>: Ask students to think about situations that have made them anxious in the past, such as making a presentation to class, the first day of attendance at a new school, asking someone out on a date, starring in the school play, playing a solo at the winter concert, etc.

<u>Step 2</u>: Ask students to think about what negative statements they were saying to themselves in these situations that made them feel more anxious. Ask them to write each situation down on paper. If it is a young student, you may want to give an example from your own life experience. Also, with young children you may prefer to have them draw pictures about what they experienced and ask them to verbally explain what it felt like rather than writing it out in a sentence.

<u>Step 3</u>: Have students identify how their negative self-talk contributed to raising their anxiety. Help them make the connection between what they were thinking and how they were feeling. Remember, anxiety is a mind/body experience.

<u>Step 4</u>: As a total class, collect the statements and replace the negative statements with positive statements. Work through at least three different situations.

<u>Step 5</u>: Make a transition to the test-taking or upcoming state mandated test experience that you

have been preparing them for. Go through the same sequence:
- identify negative self-talk
- identify why these statements increase anxiety
- identify the feelings associated with this negative self-talk
- replace the negative self-talk with positive self-talk.

I encourage teachers to write the positive and negative self-talk statements on the blackboard or chart paper so that students can read them and process them visually as well as auditorily. Refer to Chart XXXII as an example of this type of classroom chart. Note that students are asked to identify the "associated feeling" as well as "basic needs not fulfilled." Of course, teachers would have to adjust any instruction to be developmentally appropriate for their students.

Chart XXXII

Self-Talk Classroom Chart

	Negative Self-Talk Statement	Associated Feeling	Basic Need Not Fulfilled	Positive Self-Talk Statement
	"If I fail this test, others will think less of me."	Embarrassment	Sense of Belonging	"My true friends will care about me no matter how well I do."
Situation #1				
Situation #2				
Situation #3				
Situation #4				
Situation #5				
Situation #6				

Chapter 7
Post-Testing Strategies

As was stated in Chapter 4, the anxiety associated with high stakes tests unfortunately does not end when the test booklet is closed. For many test-takers the perception of failure and the associated symptoms of post traumatic test disorder actually results in higher anxiety in future test-taking situations, leading in extreme cases to test phobia.

If students' expectations (their perceptions) in most test-taking situations are consistent with their actual test performance, then the associated level of anxiety might not be as greatly affected as if their performances are inconsistent with their expectations. In other words, if students expect to fail and do, then post traumatic test anxiety continues to operate. If students expect to pass and do, then they continue to be confident approaching future tests as they have in the past. However, if students expect to pass, and fail, or expect to fail, but pass—then this greatly changes the associated anxiety either for better or worse.

Whenever the unexpected happens, it is a *wake up call* for students to more closely explore the reasons why reality was so different from what they anticipated. The use of self-reflection can assist students to sort out those factors that may have contributed to the outcome being different from their expectation. Did they underestimate or overestimate the test's difficulty? Did they prepare exceptionally well or poorly? What do they need to do more of, less of, for their next test? What would they do differently?

Regardless of the answers, the most effective strategy to combat post-test anxiety is one that is proactive and assists the test-takers in taking control over their emotional state through goal setting.

Goal Setting

Using this approach of goal setting to increase effort and raise motivation in students who are highly anxious avoids the pitfalls of the "carrot and stick" approach of behaviorism. Rather the basic needs of students are addressed, as was discussed when Choice Theory was reviewed in Chapter 4. After a student has failed or performed poorly on a test, he/she needs to set realistic goals for future tests. If the student is involved in planning and developing goals, the anxiety surrounding failure on a test can be diminished and energy becomes focused on what needs to be done—usually preparing to take the test again.

If performance on the test reveals that the student has a major deficiency in a particular content area, then goals should be directed toward improved learning of that content.

It is always best if goals are explicit and written down. Younger children will need more help in goal setting than older children and adolescents. However, they will all need the help and support of teachers, parents and friends. In school, teachers and mental health professionals can greatly help test anxious students develop and set realistic goals.

We have already covered in previous chapters how to address study skills and the emotional symptoms of test anxiety, as well as many of the other areas that could be incorporated into student goal setting. The more familiar one is with all the possible factors that contribute to test anxiety, as well as the strategies and techniques to address it, the more effective the goal setting will become.

Chart XXXIII

Test Anxiety Goal Setting

Test Outcome	Reason	Goal
"I failed the test"	"I was too nervous and made too many mistakes"	Learn strategies to reduce my high levels of test anxiety
"I failed the test"	"I did not prepare well"	Improve my study skills and habits
"I failed the test"	"I really don't understand the content"	Re-learn the material (perhaps in a different way)

Comparing Group Testing Results

Parents can play a pivotal role in recognizing that while the results of test scores are important, they are not the sole or *best* measure of a school district's worth, or of their child's worth. However, parents often place too much value on test scores, dwelling on the scores' impact on their children as well as the public's perception of their schools. Local real estate brokers also wait in anticipation for the release of the testing results. After all, the listing of comparative test scores from neighboring school districts is more than just idle gossip. It can mean a difference in real estate values since the perception of the quality of a given school district greatly impacts the value of property in the area.

Alfie Kohn talks about the listing of standardized test scores as similar to the listing of box scores in the sports section of the newspaper. Like schools with the best sports teams, schools with highest test scores are the public relations winners. Imagine if the scores of a given school district drop from one year to the next, or if a more affluent school district has lower scores than its less affluent neighbor. Heads will roll in the district office. Board of education members could lose re-election. Remember this is high stakes testing!

We should all recognize that test results can and do vary from class to class, year to year, and from school to school, because of many factors. Listed below are some of those factors, their impact, and the possible solutions that need to be considered.

Factor 1: One group (cohort) may perform better or worse than another.

Impact: Scores will vary since some cohorts of students may be better test-takers or better prepared in a particular subject area.

Solution: Because of this phenomenon, recognize that the best way to look at group test scores is collectively over time. The trend line is more important than any one year's cohort results.

Factor 2: Some schools spend more time "teaching to the test," and therefore will improve results more rapidly.

Impact: Teaching to a test can create a very narrow educational school experience. Other academic areas could be de-emphasized or sacrificed. Often art, music, and physical education are reduced, or even eliminated, during the test prep phase.

Solution: Learn more about the test before you worry about teaching to the test. If a

continued on next page...

...continued from previous page

test is a broad based assessment focusing on creative problem solving and higher order thinking skills, then teaching to the test can be positive. It just means helping the students better understand and prepare. However, if the test is primarily a "Jeopardy-like" experience, where the memorization of facts is important, then teaching to the test becomes very dangerous because it narrows the teaching and learning process to one outcome—passing the test.

Factor 3: Higher test scores in school A as compared to school B means that school A is better.

Impact: Depending on what the test measures, the test scores may or may not be an indicator of a school's (or district's) success or quality.

Solution: Once again, the key is to understand the test and what it purports to measure. It may be one indicator of a school or school district's quality, or it may not. Many factors should contribute to the assessment of a school.

Chapter 8
Developing Comprehensive Plans

After reading the last three chapters, filled with strategy after strategy, you may be wondering how to make sense of all of this information. I believe that schools, parents and kids need to develop and customize plans that work for them. My ultimate goal is for each stakeholder group to design and develop plans for high stakes tests—plans that are comprehensive enough to address the pre-testing, test-in-progress, and post-testing phases. Here's my wish list:

I would like all school districts and college administrators across the country to train their staff in the area of test anxiety. I would like all parent organizations to dedicate time to this topic each year as part of their parent training initiatives. I would like all schools to develop comprehensive plans to incorporate test anxiety awareness and reduction strategies into their test preparation efforts. And lastly, I would like every test-taker to recognize the symptoms of test anxiety and be equipped to address them when and if they arise.

It's a pretty ambitious list, but I truly hope that this book has helped raise consciousness about this topic. When

I first recognized that the issue of test anxiety was becoming a bigger and bigger problem in our society, I made the assumption that there were many useful products available on the market designed to address this issue. My assumption was wrong. There are many books, videos and audiotapes on the topic of anxiety, but virtually none specifically on test anxiety.

Furthermore, the majority of the resources and web sites about test preparation and test anxiety are tailored toward the college student, not toward elementary, middle and high school students. Other than the efforts of organizations like the Educational Testing Service (ETS), which administers the PSAT and SAT tests, little was being done to address test anxiety from 10th grade on down. So, I chose to write this book and had to draw widely from many different and diverse sources to pull together a logical, meaningful and practical guide on test anxiety. But this guide would be inadequate without a plan to infuse this information into the schools and homes of millions of test anxious kids. Allow me now to translate the information compiled in this book into concrete workable plans for your use as a classroom teacher, school administrator, college professor, parent, or test anxious kid.

Staff Training in Schools

Every year across America schools spend countless hours and money on staff development related to tests. Teachers attend endless workshops on aligning curriculum to standards as well as improving instruction in the classroom. I propose that as part of a comprehensive plan of staff development in each school district, teachers be offered a course on test anxiety. There are plenty of skilled and knowledgeable master teachers capable of leading such a course. There are also many wonderful mental health workers in the schools (school psychologists, school social workers, and guidance counselors) who are also well equipped to teach such a course to professional staff. Feel free to use this book as a guide. Pick and choose what you feel is appropriate. Adjust the content based on the ages and grade levels that the participants in such a course would be teaching. Although my sample outline parallels the content of this book, the course could be customized to the wishes and needs of the school district. The choices are optional, but offering such a course is not.

A sample staff development course outline for teachers appears in Chart XXXIV. The course could be offered after school, on a Saturday, or over the summer. But it should be an offering in the district staff development plan. Unless classroom teachers are aware of and trained to address test anxiety, it is going to continue to spiral out of control as the increased demands of the No Child Left Behind Act become fully implemented.

It is my hope that the rationale for such staff development becomes apparent to school administrators as they recognize its potential benefit to their teachers and ultimately to their students and districts. Creating school environments that anticipate and effectively address test anxiety will place those school districts on the cutting edge of test preparation. It will provide them with a comprehensive approach which incorporates the emotional as well as academic components necessary to maximize test performance...this becomes a win-win situation for all involved. Teachers will feel better prepared to help kids. Kids will be better equipped to handle the rigors of high stake tests, and school districts will benefit from higher test scores.

Chart XXXIV

Staff Development Course
(Sample Outline)

Reducing Test Anxiety in Children
(or in Adolescents)
(or in College Students)

I. What is Test Anxiety?
- Relationship to high stakes testing
- Factors that contribute to its rise
- Teaching to the test

II. Why is it a Man-Made Emotion?
- Differences between fear and anxiety
- The concept of "optimal" test anxiety
- The stakeholder groups (parents, teachers and kids)

III. What do We Know About Controlling Test Anxiety?
- Addressing the three phases (pre-test, test-in-progress, post-test)
- Understanding the related theories (i.e., Multiple Intelligences, Emotional Intelligence and Choice Theory)
- The role of differentiated instruction
- The Test Anxiety Triangle (physical, emotional and mental components)

continued on next page...

continued from previous page...

IV. <u>What Strategies and Techniques are Helpful?</u>
- Pre-Testing Strategies
    - — Sending positive messages
    - — Effective study skills and habits
    - — Taking practice tests
    - — Tutoring
- Test-in-Progress Strategies
    - — Test-taking strategies
    - — Testing modifications
    - — Techniques to reduce physical symptoms (i.e., deep breathing, progressive muscle relaxation, physical exercise)
    - — Techniques to reduce emotional symptoms (i.e., visualization, meditation, self-expression, use of surveys and questionnaires)
    - — Techniques to reduce mental/cognitive symptoms (i.e., positive self-talk)
- Post-Testing Strategies
    - — Goal setting
    - — Comparing group testing results

V. <u>How to Comprehensively Plan</u>
- Types of training
- Building teams
- Awareness, knowledge and action

Parent Training

Since we know that the home environment can be a major source of test anxiety for students, parent-teacher organizations need to raise awareness and take the lead. I propose that, working with school officials, parents be offered workshops (on an annual basis) on the effects of test anxiety and their contributions to it as parents.

I offer a sample parent training workshop outline in Chart XXXV that varies from the sample teacher course outline in several ways. First, the parent course should be less technical with more time spent on creating an optimal environment and less time spent on issues such as differentiated instruction, test-taking skills and other classroom related strategies. The focus should be on their role, as parents, in increasing or decreasing test anxiety in their children. A review of the types of parenting styles might open some eyes.

Second, parents should be made aware of the selected strategies that can be very helpful at home, such as those related to improving study skills and habits as well as those related to reducing the physical and emotional symptoms of test anxiety.

Third, parents need to understand that testing is a way of life in schools—from elementary school through graduate school. So the effort that we all put in together (schools, parents and kids) is a worthwhile investment. If parents set a positive, supportive emotional climate while their children are young, there will be fewer problems with test anxiety as their children get older.

Chart XXXV

Parent Training Workshop
(Sample Outline)

Test Anxiety: What Parents Can Do About It

I. What is Test Anxiety?
- The differences between fear and anxiety
- The role of high stakes tests
- The concept of "optimal" test anxiety

II. How do Parents Contribute to Test Anxiety?
- The beliefs that parents hold about tests
- Types of anxious parents
  - The Worrier
  - The Critic
  - The Victim
  - The Perfectionist

III. How can We Better Understand Test Anxiety?
- Pre-Testing Phase
- Test-in-Progress Phase
- Post-Testing Phase
- The Anxiety Triangle
  - Physical component
  - Emotional component
  - Mental/cognitive component

continued on next page...

continued from previous page...

IV. **What Strategies and Techniques are Helpful?**
- Pre-Testing Strategies
  - — Positive messages
  - — Effective study skills and habits
  - —Tutoring
- Test-in-Progress Strategies
  - — Techniques to reduce physical symptoms (i.e., deep breathing and progressive muscle relaxation)
  - — Techniques to reduce emotional symptoms (i.e., visualization and self-expression)
  - — Techniques to reduce mental/cognitive symptoms (i.e., positive self-talk)
- Post-Testing Strategies
  - — Goal setting
  - — Comparing group testing results

V. **How can Parents and Teachers Work Together?**
- Joint planning and preparation
- Increasing awareness and knowledge
- Parent/teacher/student training

Student Training

Our third stakeholder group, the kids themselves, need to be taught the strategies covered in Chapters 5, 6 and 7. However, kids cannot assume that their school (or college) will provide this help in a readily available fashion. Therefore, students who are old enough and capable enough to do so should teach themselves how to cope with test anxiety. It is definitely harder to "go it alone," but until schools and parents make the commitment to include test anxiety as a critical component in their test preparation efforts, older students cannot afford to wait. Just ask many test anxious adults who failed or did poorly on important tests related to securing a position or as a prerequisite to a job promotion. They will tell you that they should have addressed their test anxiety years ago and wish they had done so.

In addition to reading this book, older students can visit the web sites listed in Appendix C as well as select from the resources provided in the bibliography. Remember that whatever students choose to do will fulfill one or more of their basic needs.

Schoolwide Planning

Over the last six years, schools have significantly expanded their efforts to improve safety. In response to an increase in student violence in general, as well as to tragedies such as Columbine, virtually all schools have created school safety or crisis teams. Generally, these teams are comprised of a cross section of individuals representing all important constituencies in the school community, such as administrators, teachers, mental health professionals, parents, students, custodial and secretarial staff, community members and the like. The teams' goals are twofold: (1) to develop a plan to respond to a crisis or an emergency should one arise (e.g., an intruder in the school, death of a student, bomb threat, etc.), and (2) to develop and implement strategies to prevent violence and make the school a safer environment (e.g., anti-bullying programs, peer mediation, conflict resolution, building access and visitor procedures, etc.).

I believe that a testing team, like a building level safety team or committee, should be created in each school and should include a small, targeted group of individuals including the building principal or assistant principal, a teacher, a parent, a student (where appropriate) and a school mental health professional. This team's task would be to plan and inform about high stakes tests and test anxiety in the school. And, like building safety teams, the team would identify prevention strategies.

Examples of some of the responsibilities that such a team might assume include:

- Dissemination of information about tests to staff, students and parents (i.e., dates, times, locations, etc.)
- Coordination of preparation efforts with parent groups and/or test prep centers in the community (e.g., planning a PTA meeting on testing, contracting with a private test prep center to offer a course at the school, etc.)
- Development and planning of staff, parent and/or student training on test anxiety (as I explained earlier in this chapter)
- Development of response plans for highly anxious and/or special needs students identified in the building (e.g., individual counseling, creating support groups, teaching specific anxiety reducing techniques, offering tutoring, etc.)
- General coordination of the school's efforts to prepare students for the upcoming test (e.g., offering an SAT prep course after school, offering a study skills class, making practice tests available on the school's web site, etc.)
- Planning of how the test results will be disseminated after the test is scored (and dealing with

students with post traumatic test disorder).

Such a test preparation team could also examine ways to foster self-expression so that those students in the school who may be test anxious become known to the professionals who can in turn help them.

If an administrator does not want to create another team or committee such as I am proposing, he/she could add some of these preparation and test anxiety responsibilities to the building's case conference team. This team referred to in different states by different names (i.e., child study team, instructional support team, pupil evaluation team, pupil support team, etc.) is the group within the school that problem solves when a student is presenting a learning or behavioral problem. Although these teams function differently from school to school, the most effective ones are those which are strength-based and develop what are called pre-referral strategies—strategies designed to help the student and his/her teacher(s) in the general education environment and to prevent referral to a more restrictive special education environment.

These case conference teams can be adapted to address test anxious students either on a case-by-case basis or on a schoolwide basis. How a particular school structures key individuals to work together to address test preparation and test anxiety is not important. What is important is that each school develops a plan with the involvement of key stakeholders and that the planning process be comprehensive in scope. This plan must:

- Address all three phases of the testing process—
  the pre-testing, the test-in-progress, as well as the
  post-testing phases.

- Acknowledge the roles and encourage the involvement of all three of the stakeholder groups— teachers, parents and kids.

- Identify students who are in greatest need of support and provide opportunities for self-expression.
- Include the teaching of specific anxiety reducing strategies and techniques.

If we, as teachers, parents and kids, work together, the anxiety that has been consuming us due to increases in high stakes testing can be controlled.

Where Do We Go From Here?

I hope that I have been successful in helping you better understand test anxiety as well as its negative impact on students' emotional states and test performance. Furthermore, I hope that my common sense, easy-to-read presentation has not devalued the content in your eyes. I could have written a textbook loaded with research studies and statistics, but I truly felt that such an approach would not have reached the audience that needs to hear this message. I am now depending on you to help spread the message.

Together we must:

- **Increase awareness**—If you are a teacher, talk about test anxiety with your administrator and colleagues. If you are a parent, talk to your child's teacher and to other parents. If you are a student, talk to your teacher and to your parents. Everyone involved with high stakes testing needs to increase the awareness of test anxiety as an issue. Only through awareness can we move to the next level— understanding how to address it.

- **Increase knowledge**—Once we become aware of the important role that test anxiety plays in performance, we need to increase our knowledge of how it works and learn what we can do about it.

- **Increase communication**—We must encourage self-expression and open communication by test anxious individuals. We must also find ways to make this communication process a part of our school and home "cultures."

- **Learn and use strategies**—Once we have a solid understanding of test anxiety we must help teachers, parents and the kids learn and use specific strategies designed to control emotions and reduce the debilitating effects of test anxiety. Through goal setting and planning we can make a significant difference.

In conclusion, as we attempt to help our students in an era of increasing accountability, we must effectively address the impact of high stakes testing. No longer can the preparation for these tests be limited to drilling for content and taking endless practice tests. We must remember the comprehensive ideas included in this book and incorporate a wide range of these strategies and techniques to ensure that the negative effects of test anxiety do not lower performance.

Let's commit ourselves to no more worn erasers, broken pencils, or sleepless nights!

Appendix A

Medications Commonly Used to Treat Childhood Anxiety Disorders*

Serotonin Reuptake Inhibitors (SRI)

SRIs are the most commonly used medications now for child and adolescent anxiety disorders, in that they can be effective, have a better side effect profile than other medications, and some can be used effectively even in very small dose amounts in liquid form. Typically, when effective, which may take days or weeks to be apparent, they tend to be continued for months or longer. Possible side effects include problems sleeping, irritability and impulsivity, physical discomfort or fidgetiness. The SRI's include Celexa (citalopram, escitalpram), Paxil (paroxetine), Prozac (fluoxetine), Luvox (fluvoxamine), and Zoloft (setraline). Effexor (venlafaxine), a type of SRI, can also be an option.

Benzodiazepines (BZ)

The BZs are usually used in the short term, to address situations that are time limited or specific to a particular anxiety-producing context, and to provide immediate assistance until a medication such as an SRI becomes effective. BZs are not typically prescribed over the long term, as they do have the potential to induce dependency or addiction, especially in

* listed in order of generally accepted preference, described only relative to anxiety disorders, may be effective for other disorders, not a complete inclusion or exclusion list.

higher doses, and can also promote labile mood and impulsive behavior. The most common side effect is fatigue, or drowsiness, a benefit if sleep induction is desired. Shorter acting BZs are most commonly used, such as Xanax (alprazolam), in one or more daily doses. Occasionally other BZs may be used, such as Ativan (lorazepam), a medium lasting BZ, and Klonopin (clonazepam), a long acting BZ. Valium (diazepam) or Halcion (triazolam) are occasionally used.

Tricyclic Antidepressants (TCA)

TCAs are less used, though they can be effective, chiefly because of their side effect profile, which, though usually not problematic, may consist of dry mouth, blurred vision, dizziness, or stomach upset. In higher doses, they can be cardiotoxic, and must be monitored by periodic blood work and EKGs. They are especially effective for panic disorder, and agoraphobia (fear of being in open or crowded places). Examples of TCAs most commonly used are Pamelor (nortryptaline) and Tofranil (imipramine). Because of a less desirable side effect profile, Norpramin (desipramine) is less used.

Beta Blockers

Technically anti-hypertensives, Beta Blockers can sometimes be used ongoing or situationally, and can be helpful. Side effects may include excessive lowering of blood pressure or pulse, sweating, dizziness. Examples are Inderal (propanolol), Corgard (nadolol), and Tenormin (atenolol).

Other Medication Options

Alpha agonists (antihypertensives) such as Tenex (guanfacine) or Catapres (clonidine) can be helpful. Buspar (buspirone), as well as Wellbutrin (bupropion) can sometimes be effective. In addition, situational dosing with antihistamine medications like Benadryl and Atarax can be helpful, though they tend to be used at night because they induce fatigue or drowsiness.

Mao Inhibitors, while effective for anxiety disorders, are not usually used with children, because of the side effect profile, with dietary restrictions that are difficult, if not impossible to implement for children.

Indirect Effects on Anxiety Symptoms

Medications such as the stimulants, like Ritalin, Methylin, Metadate, and Concerta (which have methylphenidate) or Adderall and Dexedrine (which have amphetamine) can indirectly reduce anxiety in that their "calming" effect is to promote attention and on-task behavior, by reducing disorganization, impulsivity, and off-task behavior.

Appendix B

Anxiety and Nutrition

Nutrition can play an important role in controlling anxiety. Certain foods and substances can exacerbate stress and anxiety, such as:

Foods with caffeine—because caffeine has a stimulating effect on the body, it is best to reduce the intake of coffee, tea, cola beverages and chocolate. Unfortunately, individuals consume large amounts of caffeine drinks in order to stay up late at night "cramming" for the next day's test.

Foods with preservatives—although the direct link between chemical additives and anxiety has not been clearly established, it may be wise to limit your intake of foods with artificial preservatives such as nitrates, nitrites, monosodium glutamate (MSG), BHT, BHA, as well as artificial colorings.

Foods with hormones—many animals raised for slaughter are fed hormones (such as DES) to gain weight. While these hormones have not been conclusively linked to harmful effects, they put great stress on the animals. It may therefore be prudent to avoid hormone-fed red meat, pork and poultry.

Foods with excessive salt—salty foods can affect blood pressure and reduce the body's supply of potassium which is an important mineral to the central nervous system.

Foods with sugar—hypoglycemia, a condition marked by a sudden drop in blood sugar levels, can mimic symptoms of anxiety (i.e., light-headedness, weakness, irritability, etc.). Therefore, it is important to not consume large amounts of sugar (particularly refined sugar) that may lead to imbalances in glucose levels. Stress can also contribute to a reduction in blood sugar levels.

Supplements—certain vitamins, such as B vitamins (B1, B2, B6, and B12), have been associated with central nervous system functioning. Vitamin C has also been known to help the body's ability to cope with stress due to its support of the adrenal glands.

St. John's Wort and Herbal Medicines—herbs such as Hypericum (St. John's Wort) have been used for years as an antidepressant. Kava and valerian act as tranquilizers. There has been a growing acceptance by the established medical community of these "alternative" medicines. Herbal supplements should be used with caution because they are not FDA approved and many have not been fully researched. Dosage issues, as well as the purity of the herb varies from country to country, as well as from manufacturer to manufacturer.

Appendix C

College Web Sites on Test Anxiety

University of California,
Irvine
www.counseling.uci.edu

Utah State University
www.usu.edu

Brigham Young University
www.byu.edu

University of Texas
www.utexas.edu

University at Buffalo
www.buffalo.edu

University of St. Thomas
www.stthomas.edu

The University of Western
Ontario
www.sdc.uwo.ca

University of Florida
(counseling center)
www.counsel.ufl.edu

State University of New York
at Potsdam
www.potsdam.edu

Glossary

Achievement Test: An assessment designed to measure an individual's degree of accomplishment or learning in a subject area. Usually a norm-referenced instrument.

Alignment: The extent to which a curriculum matches the standards for which it was designed. Also, the extent to which a test matches the curriculum.

Anxiety: A total mind/body response (physical, emotional and mental) to a perceived threat.

Authentic Assessment: The type of assessment that directly measures the skill area being evaluated. Sometimes referred to as "real life" assessment.

Bodily-Kinesthetic Intelligence: The capacity to skillfully use one's own body as a means of expression.

Brain-Based Learning: A type of learning based on brain research and neuroscience.

Choice Theory: A theory of human emotion and behavior developed by William Glasser; a non-controlling psychology that gives freedom to sustain relationships.

Cohort: A defined group (of students) who remain together over time.

Deep Breathing: A method of relaxing the body when one is anxious or under stress.

Diagnostic Test: A measurement designed to determine relative strengths and weaknesses, and to help prescribe a course of action.

Differentiated Instruction: A comprehensive instructional approach to effectively address the diverse learning needs of a wide range of students in a classroom environment.

Emotional Intelligence (EI): A theory of intelligence that focuses on the ability to manage and regulate emotions; developed by Peter Salovey and Jack Mayer.

Essay-Type Items: The type of test items that require a written response.

Existential Intelligence: A proposed multiple intelligence that relates to the meaning of life (e.g., spirituality and meta-physical speculations).

Fear: The body's physical, emotional and cognitive response to a real danger or threat.

Fill-in-the-Blank Items: The type of test item that requires a single word (or phrase) response, usually to complete a sentence.

Graphic Aids: Any type of aid that displays information in a visual or pictorial manner (e.g. pie charts, graphs and picto-graphs).

Graphic Organizers: Visual display or dipiction of material that facilitates its clarification, understanding and retention (e.g. web and flow charts).

High Stakes Testing: Norm-referenced testing for which a significant outcome is dependent on the results (e.g., grade promotion or retention; college admission; state funding, etc.); usually part of a state or nationally developed system.

Individuals with Disabilities Education Act (IDEA): The federal legislation which governs the education of students with disabilities ages 3-21.

Interpersonal Intelligence: The capacity to effectively respond to other people and understand their feelings.

Intrapersonal Intelligence: The capacity to know one's self, including one's own strengths, motivations, goals and feelings.

Linguistic Intelligence: The capacity to use language as a means of expression and communication.

Logical/Mathematical Intelligence: The capacity to think logically, use numbers effectively and solve problems scientifically.

Matching Items: The type of test items requiring a match between two separate bits of information.

Meditation: A method of relaxation; the act of thinking about something deeply and carefully to aid in relaxation.

Multiple Choice Items: The type of test items consisting of a "stem" (in a question-format or incomplete sentence) followed by a choice of possible answers (usually 4 or 5).

Mental Health Professionals: A term for individuals in the "helping" professions, such as psychologists, social workers, therapists, and counselors.

Multiple Intelligences: A psychological theory of intelligence based on the work of Howard Gardner; it argues that individuals can be intelligent across a wide variety of domains.

Musical Intelligence: The capacity to appreciate and use music and musical forms as a vehicle of expression.

Naturalist Intelligence: The capacity to understand, relate and explain things encountered in the world of nature.

No Child Left Behind (NCLB) Act: The federal legislation, passed in 2002, which governs elementary and secondary education.

Norm-Referenced Test: A test that has been statistically standardized to a representative sample of examinees; results are interpreted with respect to a norm.

Objective Test: An assessment where results can be scored against a pre-determined standard. Answers are either right or wrong, and the scores are quantifiable.

Portfolio: A collection of work samples that represent an individual's performance in a given subject or skill.

Positive Self-Talk: A strategy for changing irrational thinking (using faulty logic) into positive and rational statements.

Post-Testing Phase: The time period that extends from the completion of a test until its test results are reported.

Post Traumatic Stress Disorder: Heightened stress and anxiety evidenced after a traumatic event.

Post Traumatic Test Disorder: Anxiety associated with the perceptions of failure after the completion of a test.

Pre-Testing Phase: The period extending from the announcement of a test until its administration. During this time most test anxiety strategies and techniques are taught and practiced.

Progressive Muscle Relaxation: A strategy relaxing the body by tensing and relaxing muscles in a sequential order.

Rubric: A means of evaluating and scoring student work that involves clear, pre-established criteria and gradations of quality.

Section 504: A section of the 1973 federal Rehabilitation Act that addresses the rights of individuals with disabilities.

Self-Expression: The ability to communicate one's feelings and emotions to others.

Spatial Intelligence: The capacity to think visually and orient oneself spatially.

Stakeholder Groups: A group that holds a vested interest in an activity such as high stakes testing. Parents, teachers and kids are stakeholders.

Standardized Test: A test that has been constructed and administered with standard directions and under standard conditions; the test and its scoring system is developed on a representative sample.

State-Mandated Test: A standardized test developed and administered by a state authority, designed to measure achievement or performance.

Study Habits: Those habits or routines that enhance the ability of a learner to benefit from study.

Study Skills: Those skills that assist in the preparation, understanding, retention and recall of previously learned material.

Subjective Test: An instrument designed without a predetermined set of absolute correct or incorrect answers; one that is not standardized or norm-referenced.

Testing Modifications: A range of accommodations utilized by students with disabilities during the administration of a test (i.e., extension of time limits).

Test-in-Progress Phase: The period extending from just before a test is begun until its completion.

Visualization: A method of relaxation involving imagining peaceful places and scenarios.

Bibliography

Armstrong, Thomas. *7 Kinds of Smart: Identifying and Developing Your Many Intelligences, Revised.* New York, NY: Plume (The Penguin Group), 1999.

Armstrong, Thomas. *Beyond the ADD Myth: Classroom Strategies and Technigues* (Video). Port Chester, NY: National Professional Resources, Inc., 1996.

Armstrong, Thomas. *Multiple Intelligences: Discovering the Giftedness in All* (Video). Port Chester, NY: National Professional Resources, Inc., 1997.

Armstrong, Thomas. *Multiple Intelligences in the Classroom, 2nd Edition.* Alexandria, VA: ASCD Publications, 2000.

Armstrong, Thomas. *The Myth of the ADD Child.* New York, NY: Plume (The Penguin Group), 1995.

Bender, William. *Differentiating Instruction for Students with Learning Disabilities.* Thousand Oaks, CA: Corwin Press, 2002.

Benson, Herbert. *The Relaxation Response.* New York, NY: Morrow, 1975.

Benson, Herbert. *Beyond the Relaxation Response.* New York, NY: Berkley Books, 1985.

Bocchino, Rob. *Emotional Literacy: To be a Different Kind of Smart.* Thousand Oaks, CA: Corwin Press, 1999.

Bourne, Edmund. *The Anxiety and Phobia Workbook, 3rd Edition.* Oakland, CA: New Harbinger Publications, 2000.

Brenner, A. *Helping Children Cope With Stress.* San Francisco, CA: New Lexington Press, 1984.

Brown, J. L. *No More Monsters in the Closet: Teaching Your Children to Overcome Everyday Fears and Phobias.* New York, NY: Prince, 1995.

Claman, Cathy (editor). *10 Real SATs, 2nd Edition.* Forrester Center, WV: College Board Publications, 2000.

Cohen, Jonathan (editor). *Educating Hearts and Minds: Social Emotional Learning and the Passage into Adolescence.* New York, NY: Teachers College Press, 1999.

Curtis, J. & Detert, R. *How to Relax.* New York, NY: HarperCollins, 1998.

Dacey, John and Fiore, Lisa. *Your Anxious Child: How Parents and Teachers Can Relieve Anxiety in Children.* New York, NY: Jossey-Bass, 2000.

DuPont, R. L., Spencer, E. D., and DuPont, C. M. *The Anxiety Cure: An Eight-Step Program for Getting Well.* New York, NY: Wiley, 1998.

Feldman-Barrett, L., & Salovey, P. (Eds.). *The Wisdom in Feeling: Psychological Processes in Emotional Intelligence.* New York, NY: Guilford Press, 2002.

Gardner, Howard. *Frames of Mind: The Theory of Multiple Intelligences* (10th Anniversary Edition). New York, NY: Basic Books, 1993.

Gardner, Howard. *How Are Kids Smart? Multiple Intelligences in the Classroom* (Video). Port Chester, NY: National Professional Resources, Inc., 1995.

Gardner, Howard. *Intelligence Reframed.* New York, NY: Basic Books, 1999.

Gardner, Howard. *Multiple Intelligences: The Theory in Practice.* New York, NY: Basic Books, 1992.

Gardner, Howard. *The Disciplined Mind.* New York, NY: Basic Books, 2000.

Gardner, Howard. *The Unschooled Mind: How Children Think and How Schools Should Teach.* New York, NY: Basic Books, 1991.

Gerzon, R. *Finding Serenity in the Age of Anxiety.* New York, NY: Bantam Books, 1998.

Glasser, William. *Choice Theory: A New Psychology of Personal Freedom.* New York, NY: HarperCollins, 1998.

Glasser, William. *Reality Therapy in Action.* New York, NY: HarperCollins, 2000.

Glasser, William. *Schools Without Failure.* New York, NY: HarperCollins, 1975.

Glasser, William. *The Quality School: Managing Students Without Coercion, 2nd Edition.* New York, NY: HarperCollins, 1998.

Goleman, Daniel. *Emotional Intelligence: A New Vision for Educators* (Video). Port Chester, NY: National Professional Resources, Inc., 1996.

Goleman, Daniel. *Emotional Intelligence: Why it Matters More Than IQ.* New York, NY: Bantam Books, 1995.

Green, Sharon Weiner and Wolf, Ira K. *Barron's How to Prepare for the SAT I, 21st Edition.* Hauppauge, NY: Barron's Educational Series, 2001.

Gregory, Gale and Chapman, Carolyn. *Differentiated Instructional Strategies: One Size Doesn't Fit All.* Thousand Oaks, CA: Corwin Press, 2002.

Hallowell, E. M. Worry: *Hope and Help for a Common Condition.* New York, NY: Ballantine Books, 1997.

Hanson, Helene and Iervolino, Constance. *Differentiated Instructional Practice Video Series: A Focus on Inclusion (Tape 1), A Focus on the Gifted (Tape 2).* Port Chester, NY: National Professional Resources, Inc. 2003.

Hart, Leslie. *Human Brain and Human Learning.* Kent, WA: Books for Educators, 1998.

Heacox, Diane. *Differentiated Instruction: How to Reach and Teach All Learners (Grades 3-12).* Minneapolis, MN: Free Spirit Press, 2002.

Hunter, Madeline. *Improved Instruction.* El Segundo, CA: TIP Publications, 1976.

Hunter, Madeline. *Mastery Teaching.* El Segundo, CA: TIP Publications, 1982.

Jensen, Eric. *Brain-Based Learning, Revised.* San Diego, CA: The Brain Store, 2000.

Jensen, Eric. *Successful Applications of Brain-Based Learning* (Two video set). Port Chester, NY: National Professional Resources, Inc., 2000.

Jersild, A. & Holmes, F. "Children's Fears Child Development". *Monograph* No. 20, 1935.

Kohn, Alfie. *Beyond the Standards Movement: Defending Quality Education in an Age of Test Scores* (Video). Port Chester, NY: National Professional Resources, Inc., 2000.

Kohn, Alfie. *Punished by Rewards*. New York, NY: Houghton Mifflin, 1993.

Kohn, Alfie. *The Case Against Standardized Testing: Raising the Scores, Ruining the Schools*. Portsmouth, NH: Heinemann, 2000.

Kohn, Alfie. *The Schools Our Children Deserve*. New York, NY: Houghton Mifflin, 1999.

LeDoux, Joseph. *The Emotional Brain*. New York, NY: Simon & Schuster, 1996.

Levine, Mel. *A Mind at a Time*. New York, NY: Simon & Schuster, 2002.

Levine, Mel. *Developing Minds Multimedia Library (Videos)*. Boston, MA: WGBH, 2001.

Manassis, K. *Keys to Parenting Your Anxious Child*. New York, NY: Barron's, 1996.

Mangrum, Charles, Iannuzzi, Patricia and Strichart, Stephen. *Teaching Study Skills and Strategies in Grades 4-8*. Needham Heights, MA: Allyn & Bacon, 1998.

Mayer, J.D., Salovey, P. and Caruso, D. *Emotional intelligence as Zeitgeist, as personality, and as a mental ability*. In R. Bar-On and J.D.A. Parker (Eds.) *The Handbook of Emotional Intelligence* (pp. 92-117). San Francisco, CA: Jossey-Bass, 2000.

Mayer, J.D., Salovey, P. and Caruso, D. *Models of emotional intelligence*. In R.J. Sternberg (Ed.), *The Handbook of Intelligence* (pp.396-420). New York, NY: Cambridge University Press, 2000.

Mayer, J.D., Caruso, D. and Salovey, P. *Selecting a measure of emotional intelligence: The case for ability scales.* In R. Bar-On and J.D.A. Parker (Eds.) *The Handbook of Emotional Intelligence* (pp.320-342). San Francisco, CA: Jossey-Bass, 2000.

Mayer, J.D., Salovey, P. and Caruso, D. *The Mayer-Salovey-Caruso Emotional Intelligence Test (MSCEIT).* Toronto, ON: MultiHealth Systems, 2001.

Pert, Candace. *Emotion: Gatekeeper to Performance* (Video). Port Chester, NY: National Professional Resources, Inc., 1999.

Pert, Candace. *Molecules of Emotion.* New York, NY: Scribner, 1997.

Sacks, Peter. *Standardized Minds.* Cambridge, MA: Perseus Publishing, 1999.

Salovey, P., & Sluyter, D. (Eds.). *Emotional Development and Emotional Intelligence: Implications for Educators.* New York, NY: Basic Books, 1997.

Schumm, Jeanne Shay and Schumm, Gerald. *The Reading Tutor's Handbook.* Minneapolis, MN: Free Spirit Publishing, 1999.

Shaw, M. A. Your Anxious Child: *Raising a Healthy Child in a Frightening World.* New York, NY: Birch Lane Press, 1995.

Strichart, Stephen and Mangrum, Charles. *Teaching Learning Strategies and Study Skills.* Boston, MA: Allyn & Bacon, 2002.

Suinn, R. "Anxiety and Cognitive Dissonance", *Journal of General Psychology*, 73, 113, 1965.

Teele, Sue. *Rainbows of Intelligence: Exploring How Students Learn.* Thousand Oaks, CA: Corwin Press, 1999.

Teele, Sue. *Rainbows of Intelligence: Raising Student Performance Through Multiple Intelligences* (Video). Port Chester, NY: National Professional Resources, Inc., 2000.

Tomlinson, Carol Ann. *How to Differentiate Instruction in Mixed-Ability Classroooms, 2nd Edition.* Alexandria, VA: ASCD, 2001.

Wilson, Reid. *Don't Panic: Taking Control of Anxiety Attacks (Revised Edition).* New York, NY: HarperCollins, 1996.

Wolfe, Patricia. *Brain Matters: Translating Research into Classroom Practice.* Alexandria, VA: ASCD, 2001.

Index

A

accessing information, 117
acronyms, 116
acrostic sentences, 116
ADD/ADHD, 34
aerobic exercise, 150
alignment, 11
amygdala, 74
anxiety, 19-24
    optimal, 27-29, 41
    test,
assessments
    authentic, 12
    types of, 47
attribution, 85

B

Benson, H., 156
blame the child syndrome, 33-35
blame the school syndrome, 35-36
bodily-kinestethic intelligence, 66
Bourne, E., 39, 40, 156
brain-based learning, 73-74

C

Chapman, C., 64
choice theory, 87-89, 91, 184
cohort, 179
C.O.P.E. method, 167-168

D

Dacey, J., 167-168
Davis, M., 74
deep breathing, 144-147
differentiated instruction, 63-64, 91

E

emotional component, 78
Emotional Intelligence, 70-73, 91
emotions
    and the brain, 73-74
English language learners (ELL), 162
environments, the, 26-27, 73
essay-type items, 137-141
existential intelligence, 67

F

fear, 19-24
fill-in-the-blank items, 135
Fiore, L., 167-168

G

Gardner, H., 65-66, 68-69, 71
Glasser, W., 87-89
goal setting, 176-177
Goleman, D., 71-73
graphic organizers, 112-114, 139
Gregory, G., 64

H

Heacox, D., 64
high stakes testing, 3, 41, 85, 122
Hunter, M., 50-52

I

individal's characteristics
    an, 24-25, 82
Individuals with Disabilities
    Education Act (IDEA), 15
interpersonal intelligence, 67, 68
intrapersonal intelligence, 67, 68

ADDITIONAL MATERIALS PUBLISHED/PRODUCED BY NATIONAL PROFESSIONAL RESOURCES, INC.

~ VIDEOS ~

Emotional Intelligence: A New Vision for Educators

Daniel Goleman

Drawing on groundbreaking research, Goleman shows that Emotional Intelligence is more important than IQ. Research indicates that our emotions play a much greater role in decision-making and individual success than has been commonly acknowledged. Join Dan Goleman and educators from the New Haven, CT Public Schools and The Nueva School in California as they effectively implement Emotional Intelligence. Find out what we can do as educators to effectively incorporate Emotional Intelligence into our classrooms.
VHS, 40 minutes   Order # VEIN-TEST $89.95
Also available with Spanish subtitles
Order # VEIS-TEST $99.95

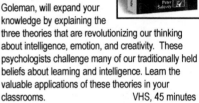

Optimizing Intelligences: Thinking, Emotion & Creativity

This exciting video, hosted by Peter Salovey and featuring Mihaly Csikszentmihalyi, Howard Gardner, and Daniel Goleman, will expand your knowledge by explaining the three theories that are revolutionizing our thinking about intelligence, emotion, and creativity. These psychologists challenge many of our traditionally held beliefs about learning and intelligence. Learn the valuable applications of these theories in your classrooms.   VHS, 45 minutes
Order #VOPI-TEST (Closed Captioned) $99.95
Also available with Spanish subtitles
Order # VOPS-TEST $109.95

How Are Kids Smart? Multiple Intelligences in the Classroom

Howard Gardner

Learn about MI theory, and observe first hand how teachers have incorporated MI theory into their teaching, classrooms and community. No longer do we ask "How smart are our kids?" but "How are kids smart?" A must for every classroom teacher struggling with the challenges of increasing diversity, inclusion of students with special needs and the move toward heterogeneous grouping.

Teachers Version, VHS, 31 minutes	Order #VMIT-TEST	$69.00
Administrators Version, VHS, 41 minutes	Order #VKSA-TEST	$99.00
Also available with Spanish subtitles	Order # VKST-TEST	$79.00

Differentiated Instruction Practice Video Series

To better meet the needs of today's diverse students, National Professional Resources, Inc. is proud to present the **Differentiated Instructional Practice Series** (DIPS). Each video in this series focuses on a specific population of students who present a unique challenge in contemporary classrooms. Learn how you can differentiate your classroom or train others to differentiate theirs, by observing the teaching and learning process in real classrooms, K-12. Accompanying each video is a **Viewer's Guide.**

Tape 1 - Differentiated Instruction: A Focus on Inclusion

Targets customized practices that are most effective in classrooms where special education students are fully included.   2003, VHS, 50 minutes
Order # VDIF1-TEST $129.00

Tape 2 - Differentiated Instruction: A Focus on the Gifted

Targets customized practices that are most effective in classrooms that seek to challenge gifted/high achieving students.   2003, VHS, 50 minutes
Order # VDIF2-TEST $129.00

Buy the Series and SAVE!! ~ Only $199 for both tapes. Order # VDIF3-TEST

~ BOOKS ~

The Power of Social Skills in Character Development: Helping Diverse Learners Succeed

Jennifer L. Scully

This book gives you 80 powerful, classroom-tested lesson plans. A complete program for helping your students gain self-esteem and improve relationships with peers, teachers and adults outside of school.
2000, soft cover, 198 pages
Order # PSSC-TEST $29.95

Engaging the Resistant Child Through Computers: A Manual to Facilitate Social & Emotional Learning

Maurice J. Elias, Ph.D., Brian S. Friedlander, Ph.D. & Steven E. Tobias, Psy.D.

This book is written for practicing clinicians, school psychologists, social workers, guidance counselors, teachers, and others who work with children (preschoolers through adolescence).
2001, soft cover, 185 pages
Order # UCER-TEST $39.95

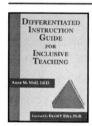

Differentiated Instruction Guide for Inclusive Teaching

Anne M. Moll, Ed.D.

Focuses on the specific questions and corresponding actions teachers must take for differentiating instruction in the general education curriculum <u>for students with disabilities **AND** for all other students who are experiencing difficulty learning</u>. It gives general and special education teachers, instructional supervisors, and members of the IEP Team explicit steps for ensuring that students have access to the general education curriculum-regardless of the envirnoment where they receive services.
2003, soft cover, approx. 160 pages
Order # DIGIT-TEST $29.95

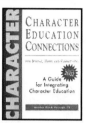

Character Education Connections: For School, Home & Community - A Guide for Integrating Character Education

D. Stirling, G. Archibald, L. McKay & S. Berg

This is a clear, concise, holistic resource for classroom teachers with a thoughtful collection of approaches to integrating character education into daily learning and school life. Well-written and organized, it provides an excellent overview of the field with a wealth of specific, field-tested plans for every level from K – 12.
2002, soft cover, 344 pages
Order #CECA-TEST $39.95

Character and Coaching: Building Virtue in Athletic Programs

J.M. Yeager, A.L. Baltzell, J.N. Buxton, & W.B. Bzdell

This book is written **for** coaches **by** coaches. The authors collective experience - as athletes, coaches, and program directors from all levels, youth programs to professional athletics - creates a resource with a depth and practicality that sets it apart from other works in the field.
2001, soft cover, 194 pages
Order # CHCO-TEST $24.95

About the Author

Dr. Joseph Casbarro has worked as an educator for thirty years in public schools, including administrative positions as building principal, director of special programs, and assistant superintendent of schools.

Dr. Joseph Casbarro

He received his Ph.D. from Syracuse University in School Psychology and has taught for many years at both the undergraduate and graduate levels.

Dr. Casbarro's interest in writing on test anxiety was a combination of his training and experiences as a psychologist, his observations of the impact of high stakes testing on schools as an administrator, and the personal experiences of his two school-age children as a parent.

If you would like to contact the author, he can be reached via e-mail at: testanxiety@NPRinc.com.

Notes

Notes

Notes